Hollywood's Star-Crossed Blonde
Carole Lombard, Marilyn Monroe, and ...

By Charles River Editors

About Charles River Editors

Charles River Editors provides superior editing and original writing services across the digital publishing industry, with the expertise to create digital content for publishers across a vast range of subject matter. In addition to providing original digital content for third party publishers, we also republish civilization's greatest literary works, bringing them to new generations of readers via ebooks.

Sign up here to receive updates about free books as we publish them, and visit Our Kindle Author Page to browse today's free promotions and our most recently published Kindle titles.

Introduction

Jean Harlow (1911-1937)

Publicity photo of Jean Harlow

"I wasn't born an actress. Events just made me one." – Jean Harlow

When the American Film Institute ranked its top 50 screen legends of the 20th century, many of the people named had careers spanning several decades, but one of them managed the feat despite living less than three decades. Ranked as the 22nd greatest actress of the 20th century, Jean Harlow was on the screen for less than 10 years, but in that time the "Blonde Bombshell" became the most popular actress of the 1930s, eclipsing superstars like Joan Crawford and Norma Shearer along the way. In fact, the platinum blonde accomplished that feat as a leading lady for just 5 years before her premature death of renal failure at just 26 years old.

Although Harlow is remembered today more for her tragic fate than her career, she was influential well beyond the 1930s. Despite being so young, she managed to craft a persona as a seductive femme fatale that would critically shape how subsequent actresses approached similar roles, and of course, her platinum blonde hair served as a template for future blonde bombshells like Marilyn Monroe, who actually watched Harlow's movies and studied her performances to model her own early career off the dead legend.

Hollywood's Star-Crossed Blonde Bombshells: The Lives of Jean Harlow, Carole Lombard, Marilyn Monroe, and Jayne Mansfield examines the short but influential life and career of one of America's first iconic blonde bombshells. Along with pictures of important people, places, and events, you will learn about Jean Harlow like never before.

Carole Lombard (1908-1942)

Paramount Studio picture of Carole Lombard in 1932

"Carole Lombard's tragic death means that something of gaiety and beauty have been taken from the world at a time they are needed most." – Errol Flynn

On January 16, 1942, just a few weeks after Pearl Harbor brought the United States into World War II, the nation suffered what were considered the first civilian deaths of the war when a plane crashed into the side of a mountain southwest of Las Vegas. Aboard the plane were 15 servicemen, but the plane was also carrying one of Hollywood's biggest stars: actress Carole Lombard.

Although Lombard's death and her marriage to *Gone With the Wind* star Clark Gable have overshadowed her career, her untimely death in 1942 cut short the life of one of Hollywood's most prominent stars at the time. In fact, Lombard's platinum look and her unique mannerisms had helped her become the biggest star of the screwball genre by the end of the 1930s, and her movies were so successful that she was the highest paid actress in Hollywood by the start of the 1940s. As English critic Graham Greene said of her, "Platinum blonde, with a heart-shaped face, delicate, impish features and a figure made to be swathed in silver lamé, Lombard wriggled expressively through such classics of hysteria as *Twentieth Century* and *My Man Godfrey*." Indeed, despite dying at the age of 33, the American Film Institute recognized her as one of the biggest film icons of the 20th century.

Although Lombard has been memorialized in many fitting ways as an actress, one of her biggest contributions to Hollywood was the blond archetype that the film industry used successfully for decades in screwball comedies, paving the way for the success of women like Marilyn Monroe. Perhaps the most remarkable aspect of that fact is that it was actually based on Carole's gushing personality. As famous director Howard Hawks noted of her, "She acted like a schoolgirl ... and she was stiff, she would try and imagine a character and then act according to her imaginings instead of being herself." When Lombard started simply portraying herself, Hawks told actor John Barrymore, "[Y]ou've just seen a girl that's probably going to be big a star, and if we can just keep her from acting, we'll have a hell of a picture."

Hollywood's Star-Crossed Blonde Bombshells: The Lives of Jean Harlow, Carole Lombard, Marilyn Monroe, and Jayne Mansfield examines the life and career of one of the Golden Era of Hollywood's biggest stars. Along with pictures of important people, places, and events, you will learn about Carole Lombard like never before.

Marilyn Monroe (1926-1962)

"The truth is I've never fooled anyone. I've let people fool themselves. They didn't bother to find out who and what I was. Instead they would invent a character for me. I wouldn't argue with them. They were obviously loving somebody I wasn't. When they found this out, they would blame me for disillusioning them and fooling them." – Marilyn Monroe

Few actresses lived their lives in the public eye more than Marilyn Monroe, and yet her life remains shrouded in mystery to this day. While it is common knowledge that Marilyn's life is a rags-to-riches story, her life is bookended by hazy details surrounding her early life and even more mysterious death.

Who was Norma Jean Baker? Who was Marilyn Monroe? The unknown has contributed to the mythology that has since become part of her legacy, and she nurtured it. Marilyn was adept at constructing a fanciful mystique about her early years, and it's become all but impossible to disentangle the truth from the narrative that Marilyn helped establish. Fittingly, even though Marilyn is instantly recognizable and still one of film's greatest icons, her films remain unfamiliar to the vast majority of the public.

Most people have some preconception of Marilyn's film persona, seeing her as the "dumb blonde" without a brain who existed only in order to be gazed upon. However, one of the essential questions concerning Marilyn's life involves the accuracy of the "Marilyn stereotype"; is the "dumb blonde" identity an accurate descriptor of her film roles, and how does it compare to Marilyn's personality off of the movie set? Given how famous Marilyn Monroe was and continues to be, it's remarkable that so many people know so little about her life and career.

What is known is that Marilyn Monroe was America's ultimate sex symbol in the 20th century, in part because she came of age in the wake of World War II and became famous during the conservative era of the 1950s. She appeared in just two films in the 1960s, prior to her premature death in August 1962, and there is a wide gulf between the brevity of her career and the impact that she made on American culture throughout the 1950s. Marilyn's death left everyone to speculate where her career would have gone in the 1960s, but it's probably safe to guess she wouldn't be the icon she remains today.

Hollywood's Star-Crossed Blonde Bombshells: The Lives of Jean Harlow, Carole Lombard, Marilyn Monroe, and Jayne Mansfield comprehensively examines the starlet's life and films, exploring the controversies and the ways in which her life and works are mutually informative. Along with pictures of important people, places, and events, you will learn about Marilyn Monroe like you never have before.

Jayne Mansfield (1933-1967)

Jayne Mansfield with Johnny Longden, Eddie Arcaro and Willie Shoemaker at the Jockeys' Ball in Los Angeles (1957)

"I don't know why you people like to compare me to Marilyn or that girl, what's her name, Kim Novak. Cleavage, of course, helped me a lot to get where I am. I don't know how they got there." – Jayne Mansfield

Although she came of age in an era when Hollywood studios were looking for blonde bombshells like Marilyn Monroe, and she followed that path to instant stardom, Jayne Mansfield had one of the most unique Hollywood careers in the 1950s and 1960s. After getting her start on Broadway, Mansfield shot to fame in Hollywood during the late '50s with her platinum blonde hair and picturesque body, and her life became equal parts movie star and celebrity, with her appearances on film more than matched by her appearances in tabloids and Playboy.

Naturally, Mansfield was a rival of Marilyn Monroe who was used by 20th Century Fox to play the same kind of ditzy blonde roles that had made Marilyn one of the biggest stars in America, which had the effect of making her famous but not exactly critically acclaimed. It was an ironic predicament for a woman who had been a Broadway actress, and she struggled to break out of being pigeonholed as a dumb blonde, the kind of stereotype many in her position had struggled with as far back as Jean Harlow and Carole Lombard. No matter how hard she tried, the peak of her career was gone before it had practically started, and by 1960, her parent studio was looking for ways to loan her out rather than use her in its own films. As a result, Mansfield remains famous today more as a pop culture phenom and sex symbol than for her acting career.

Of course, one of the other reasons Jayne Mansfield is remembered so vividly today is the grisly nature of her tragic death. Even without movies, Mansfield was constantly in the public eye through various publicity stunts and other special performances, such as a striptease revue, and she was still just 34 years old when she was killed in a car crash. In that accident, Mansfield, her lover, and her driver were all killed in the front when their car rear-ended a truck and slid under it. Thankfully, her children, sitting in the back, suffered only minor injuries. One of her surviving children, Mariska Hargitay, has since gone on to be a well-known actress herself, including a starring role as a detective in Law & Order, Special Victims Unit.

Hollywood's Star-Crossed Blonde Bombshells: The Lives of Jean Harlow, Carole Lombard, Marilyn Monroe, and Jayne Mansfield examines the notorious life and death of one of America's biggest pop culture stars of the 1950s and 1960s. Along with pictures of important people, places, and events, you will learn about Jayne Mansfield like never before, in no time at all.

Hollywood's Star-Crossed Blonde Bombshells: The Lives of Jean Harlow, Carole Lombard, Marilyn Monroe, and Jayne Mansfield

Jean Harlow

Chapter 1: Mother's Baby

"She was always all mine." - Jean Carpenter, speaking about her daughter.

Harlean Harlow Carpenter was born on March 3, 1911, in Kansas City, Missouri. Her father, Mont Clair Carpenter, was 34 years old and had grown up on a small farm in Kansas, but as soon as he was old enough, Mont Clair had left the farm and moved to Kansas City, Kansas to seek his fortune. After working for a while in a meat packing plant, he enrolled in the Kansas City Dental College, where he graduated in 1902. He then set up a practice across the state line in Kansas City, Missouri.

Within a few years, Carpenter had a successful dental practice and was moving up in Kansas City society. It was during this time that he met Jean Poe Harlow, the daughter of a wealthy real estate speculator named Skip Harlow. For reasons that remain unclear, Skip Harlow decided that his daughter should marry Carpenter, and given that young Jean was known for being high-spirited and difficult to manage, it seems that perhaps she had done something in her life that called into question her chances of a good marriage within Kansas City society. As a result, Skip arranged for Mont Clair to marry her in 1908, and as part of the bargain he even threw in a house for the two of them to live in.

The Carpenters had a difficult marriage from the very beginning. Jean never loved her husband and had only married him to please her father, and by the time Harlean (whom the family always called "the baby" or simply "Baby") was born, Jean was thoroughly dissatisfied with her marital state. To make up for her own unhappy circumstances, she poured all her attention and affection into young Harlean; she would later tell Hollywood gossip columnist Louella Parsons that she never let her daughter wake up without finding her sitting by her bed, waiting for her eyes to open. She added, "I started when she was a tiny infant and I have never let anything interfere with my kissing her good morning as soon as she opened her eyes. Sometimes I sit for an hour watching her in her sleep."

Jean Harlow and her mother

Ultimately, Jean was simply too intelligent and ambitious to be satisfied being the proper housewife of a successful dentist, and while she was unsure of what she could do to change her own life, she was determined that young Harlean would be given more opportunities than she ever had. As a result, she enrolled her little girl at the age of five in Miss Barstow's Finishing School for Girls. Founded in 1884 by Wesley College graduates Mary Barstow and Ada Brann, the Barstow School was considered the best private school in Kansas City. Located in a four-story building on a large lot near Main Street, it boasted 150 students for whom it wanted "to promote sound scholarship and to give symmetrical development to my mind, body and character."

However, once Harlean was spending most of her days at school, Jena became even more restless and dissatisfied with her life. She filed for divorce when Harlean was 11 years old, and after the decree was granted in September 1922, she began to plan her escape from the Midwest. The following year, she and Harlean moved to Hollywood, but unlike other future stars' mothers, the move wasn't necessarily made with the young girl in mind. Though she was already 34 years old, Jean felt that she still had a chance to break into the new burgeoning movie industry herself. Sadly, she soon learned how wrong she was, because by then, Hollywood was recruiting actresses in their late teens, not middle-aged housewives. The few actresses who did play the parts of older women got them because they had already been in the business for years, so it went without saying that a newcomer like Jean Carpenter was no match for seasoned actresses like Jane Darwell and Phyliss Gordon.

While her mother was floundering, Harlean was attending the Hollywood School of Girls.

Founded in 1909 by Sophie Hogan, the school encouraged its students to develop both their minds and their bodies, and when Harlean was enrolled there in 1923, the two story stucco building on La Brea Avenue was less than 10 years old. The principal, Mrs. Louise Knappen Woolett, was an ambitious woman who eventually expanded the school's offerings to include a junior college program. While at the Hollywood School, Harlean would become friends with Irene Mayer, the future wife of David O. Selznick. She also met soon-to-be heartthrob Douglas Fairbanks, Jr.

Irene Mayer Selznick

Fairbanks, Jr.

Not surprisingly, Hollywood proved to be a very expensive place for a single mother and her daughter to live, and with no job, Jean was dependent on an allowance from her father to survive. While he had supported her initial move to the West Coast, perhaps hoping that she would get the wanderlust out of her system, he grew increasingly concerned that she seemed to have no reasonable plans for her life. In 1925, he informed her that he was cutting off his support and that, furthermore, if she did not return to Kansas City immediately, he would cut her out of his will. Thus, Jean gave up on her acting dreams and returned home to Kansas. Ironically, Skip Harlow would later nearly derail his granddaughter's movie career as well.

Once back in Kansas City, Harlean found it difficult to adjust to her quiet, Midwestern surroundings. After all, she had become accustomed to seeing her classmates driven to school in chauffeured limousines and being invited to the homes of Hollywood executives, so it was difficult for the 14 year old girl to go back to walking to school with friends and grabbing a soda at the drug store.

Hoping that a change of scenery might help her adjust, Skip Harlow arranged for her to spend the July and August of 1926 at Camp Cha-Ton-Ka in Michigamme, Michigan. According to its brochure, Cha-ton-ka offered a chance for "cheerful, well-poised and healthy" girls between the ages of 9-18 to enjoy camping, sports and the arts. The owner of the camp, Barbara Woodson Root, had built it in 1922 and insisted that each camper learn to swim well, as well as build fires and cook outdoors. Most of the girls attending camp came there from Kansas City and arrived via a special train trip that included a pleasant layover in Chicago for shopping.

For her part, Harlean found nothing pleasant about the camp, and she would later say, "That camp still remains the worst nightmare of my life. I don't know how I lived through it." In fact, she barely did. After getting off to a bad start by using poison oak leaves for toilet paper during a hike, she and another camper caught scarlet fever. According to her later recollection, they were so sick that "[e]veryone was afraid to come near us except a country doctor." Harlean's case was particularly severe and may have even damaged her kidneys, leading to the illness that would take her life years later.

When Jean learned that Harlean was ill, she caught the next train to the camp, but when she arrived, the camp director would not let her see Harlean. The physician treating the girls, Dr. Isaiah Sicotte, agreed, fully aware of the risk that the scarlet fever might spread. However, Jean would not be stopped. According to her daughter, "No director and no quarantine could have kept my mother from me. She completely ignored that woman and rowed herself across the lake to camp."

Jean stayed at the camp for three weeks until Harlean was completely well. Interviewed about the incident years later, one of the campers who shared a cabin with Harlean at that time observed, "There's nothing worse than having your mother at summer camp, especially if you had her mother." Though Jean returned to Kansas City after the crisis had passed, she still insisted on traveling back to Michigan to bring her daughter home, instead of letting her take the train back with the other girls.

Their trip home would prove to be a life changing event. During a dinner time stopover in Chicago, Jean met Marino Bello, and the two formed an instant attraction, thanks primarily to her family's wealth and his interest in getting some of it. In order to have an excuse to make trips back to Chicago to meet him, Jean enrolled Harlean in the Ferry Hall School in Lake Forest, Illinois, one of the few times in life that she blatantly put her own needs ahead of her daughter's. When Harlean entered Ferry Hall in the fall of 1926, it was thoroughly in the hands of its principal, Elouise Ruthven Tremain, and had just become independent from the nearby Lake Forest University. Over the next decade, the school's rigorous standards and success would bring it national attention and lead one Hollywood produced to tout Harlow's academic prowess publicly, proclaiming, "To be admitted to Ferry Hall was a social achievement; to graduate from the school was a scholastic accomplishment".

For Harlean, though, Ferry Hill was more like a sentence. She began by rebelling against the dress code, telling the headmistress, "I won't wear such hideous shoes; I'll go home first."

Furthermore, the future sex symbol was not particularly boy crazy, as she later recalled: "Somehow I never went through the usual youthful romances that many young girls experience. The young men I knew, with the expectation of Rod Adams, were companionable, but for me they roused no dreams of romance. In fact, I much preferred passing my week-ends with mother and Marino to having 'dates.'"

It remains a mystery exactly who this Rod Adams was, but it seems that he was definitely an older man based on the following comments she later made, "During all my school life, I had one romance. He was my hero; and it did not matter that he was over 30. I secretly promised myself that someday Rod Adams would be the man I'd marry. Then I met Charles F. McGrew." When she entered Lake Forest as a freshman, Harlean was assigned a "big sister" from the senior class, and it was through her that Harlean met a 19 year old college freshman named Chuck McGrew. Like her, McGrew came from a wealthy family background, and the two began dating in the fall of 1926.

Meanwhile, Jean was busy with her own romantic pursuits and had little time to pay attention to her daughter's activities. In January 1927, she married Marino Bello, a man she had known for less than five months. It is unclear whether or not she even told Harlean she was getting married, but either way, Harlean was not at the wedding. Her mother's marriage proved to be too much for the already mixed-up girl, and she dropped out of school a few months later to marry McGrew. The two eloped to Chicago, and Harlean would later remember, "Just to give you an idea of the solemnity of our wedding a radio next door to the justice's office was blaring 'St. Louis Blues' as we listened to the words that made us man and wife."

Two months later, McGrew turned 21 and inherited part of his share of the family fortune, and with this money in hand, the young newlyweds took a train to New York and boarded a cruise ship for California. It was a dream honeymoon for the young lovers, who walked the ship's decks hand in hand and enjoyed the scenery while sailing through the still new and exotic Panama Canal. Once in California, they moved into a comfortable bungalow in Beverly Hills and set up housekeeping together.

It was a strange situation, even by Hollywood standards. There was little Harlean McGrew, only 16 years old but living as a married woman in her own home with a 21 year old husband. Neither of them worked because they could comfortably live off the money he had inherited, so instead, they spent their nights going to parties and their days sleeping off hangovers. As Harlean would later remember, "All play and no work can be fine for a time, but I became eager for something besides fun to fill the days, and I became more and more lonely for my mother. I waited, hoping that something would happen to show me the answer to my problem."

Chapter 2: Mrs. McGrew Makes a Movie

"This was the era of sophisticated sex. Clothes were bias-cut, clinging to the body for an essentially feminine look. Dresses had low backs, low necks and low under-arms. The bust was small and natural. Jean Harlow epitomized the height of the glamour period. Hers was a deliberate, calculated look; nothing mattered as long as you were glamorous." - Edith Head, Hollywood costume designer

When she first moved to Los Angeles, Harlean met a woman named Rosalie Roy, and the two became good friends, in spite of their very different backgrounds. As far as anyone in Beverly Hills new, pretty young Mrs. McGrew was a wealthy socialite from back east, but Roy, on the other hand, was a young woman who had come to the West Coast to try to break into the movies, like so many others. Roy couldn't afford a car, so Harlean often drove her to appointments and auditions.

Roy

One day, Roy asked Harlean to give her a ride to Fox Studios, where she had an appointment about a movie role, and while she was sitting in the car waiting for her friend, Harlean looked up to see an older man gazing down on her with curiosity. He introduced himself as an executive with Fox and asked what she was doing at the studio. When Harlean explained that she was just waiting for a friend, he asked if she was interested in being an actress. Even though she assured him that she was not, he still gave her a letter of introduction to Central Casting and told her to mention his name if she stopped by.

Harlean thought the whole incident was a big joke and told Rosalie as much. Perhaps irritated that her friend had been "discovered" while she continued to pound the pavement, Roy dared Harlean to go to an audition, even betting some of her hard earn cash that she would never do it. In the meanwhile, Harlean also told her mother Jean about the offer. Unable to live so far from her baby, Jean had persuaded her husband to move to Los Angeles, and they now lived in a small home a few blocks from Chuck and Harlean. Of course, Jean was very excited to hear about the story and already imagined seeing her daughter's name in lights, so she also encouraged Harlean to try out for a role.

Between her mother's pressure and her friend's bet, Harlean decided to take a chance, so she drove over to Central Casting and signed the ledger, registering herself for work. In a move that would shape her short career, she gave her name as Jean Harlow, using her mother's first name and maiden name, an homage to the starry eyed debutante her mother had been at her age. From that day on, she would be known in Hollywood as Jean Harlow, and her mother, when her name came up at all, was known as Mother Jean.

Much to her surprise, Central Casting began to call and offer Jean work as "background" in several pictures. At first, she was too busy partying to show any interest in work, but as time went by, she began to grow bored with her lifestyle and decided to try something new. Thus, in 1928, she appeared in the silent film *Honor Bound* for the meager sum of $7 a day. Of course, only those who kept track of the picture even knew she was in it, as her name appeared nowhere in the credits, but her performance was still enough to snag her a five-year contract with Hal Roach Studios for $100 a week.

Hal Roach

In 1928, Hal Roach was a big name in Hollywood, and his Culver City studio turned out some of the finest examples of silent film era comedy. He also had some of the greatest names of the day on his payroll, including Will Rogers, The Our Gangs Kids, and Laurel & Hardy. In 1925, he dealt his closest competitor, Mack Sennett, a hard blow when he stole his best supervising director, F. Richard Jones, and with Jones' help, Roach turned out dozens of films a year. That year, he also began making the transition into "talkies," which he released through MGM.

According to Harlow, it was a wonderful time to be in Hollywood, "There was friendliness and camaraderie everywhere on that lot. Stan Laurel and Babe Hardy did everything to make me feel at ease, and I wouldn't trade my experience in those comedies for anything. I seemed to realize that I was definitely deciding the course of my life. I moved around in a constant state of surprised bewilderment so suddenly had this new life opened to me; but I was determined to make the most of it."

Roach Studios kept Harlow busy, casting her in another small, uncredited role in *Moran of the Marines*, and then to play a bathing beauty in the short film *Chasing Husbands*. 1929 also proved to be a busy year for Harlow, who she continued to appear in one picture after another. She had small, uncredited roles in *Fugitives* and *Why Be Good?*, as well as in the short subjects *Why Is a Plumber?* and *The Unkissed Man*. Though she was not known for her singing ability, she still landed a small role in *Close Harmony*.

A studio shot of Harlow from the early 1930s.

Harlow finally got her big break when she co-starred with Laurel and Hardy in the short silent film *Double Whoopee*. Though she was only listed as the "Swanky Blond," the fact that she was finally getting billing showed she was making progress. Like most silent movies, *Double Whoopee* depended on visual pranks to get laughs, and in her role, Harlow had a short but funny scene in which the bumbling duo nearly strip her naked. The three had a good rapport, and she went on to make *Liberty* with them. In this film, she was on screen for just a few minutes but played the role of a woman stuck in a cab while Laurel and Hardy try to trade pants. This is also the only movie in which she was credited as Harlean Carpenter. In her third picture with the pair, *Bacon Grabbers*, she plays a harried housewife who returns home to find her house torn asunder by repo men Laurel and Hardy, who are trying to repossess a radio that she just made a payment on.

At this point, Harlow was still only on the verge of turning 18, and while she was enjoying being at the studio every day and appearing in pictures, her young husband did not care for her new career. Fearing that she was losing him, she went to Roach's office for advice and told him that acting was "breaking up my marriage". After asking him what she could do, Roach tore up her contract and sent her home to work things out with McGrew. However, by this time,

Harlow's work at the studio was more of a symptom of the pair's problems than the actual root cause. In June, she left McGrew and moved in with Mother Jean and Bello. She would later say of that time, "We were too young and too spoiled to make a go of our marriage."

Of course, Harlow also went back to making movies, appearing in several more silent pictures before landing her first speaking part in *The Saturday Night Kid*, which starred Clara Bow, in 1929. According to one movie historian, this was a very fortunate turning point in Harlow's life: "Bow, the leading sex symbol and flapper icon of the late 1920s, was losing her grip on the box office (not to mention her waistline) and didn't want the voluptuous blonde upstart drawing attention away from her. But she and Harlow soon warmed to each other, and Bow proved to be a generous supporter of the younger actress. Still, the movie did little to advance Jean's fortunes, and she floundered in uncredited bit parts until her reputed one-time lover, actor James Hall, introduced her to a lanky, eccentric Texas millionaire who was determined to become a major Hollywood player."

Clara Bow

James Hall in *Manhattan Tower*

At that time, Hall was starring in Howard Hughes' new picture *Hell's Angels*, but Hughes' production had been plagued by bad luck from the beginning. First, he had begun filming the picture as a silent movie, only to have "talkies" become the norm before he finished, so he was now reshooting it with a soundtrack. Next, he had had numerous problems and accidents while trying to film the all-important dog fights in the air. There had even been a few fatalities, causing more setbacks and making his financial backers skittish. Most recently, he had to fire his leading lady because English-speaking audiences could not understand her thick Norwegian accent. It seems that Greta Nissen would soon join the list of silent film stars who could not make the transition to talking pictures.

When Hall saw Harlow on screen, he was sure he had found Nissen's replacement. He got in touch with her, and after introducing himself, he invited her to make a screen test for the picture. Harlow's test passed Hughes' high standards, so she got the part. In addition to the starring role in Hell's Angels, Hughes also gave Harlow a five-year contract with a salary of $100 a week. As it turned out, he made a good investment, though he would not realize it right away.

Hughes

Set during World War I, *Hell's Angels* tells the story of two brothers, both pilots and both in love (or at least in lust) with the same girl, Helen (played by Harlow). In many ways, Helen set the stage for the kind of role Harlow would become famous for; she was a bad girl and didn't mind being bad. One of her most memorable lines in the movies is the oft repeated, "Would you be shocked if I put on something more comfortable?" Another line in the film is almost prophetic in the way it mirrors both the spirit and the brevity of Harlow's life. Overcome with emotion, Helen cries out, "I wanna be free. I wanna be gay and have fun. Life's short. And I wanna live while I'm alive."

When it opened at Grumman's Chinese Theater on May 27, 1930, *Hell's Angels* received only lackluster reviews and lower than expected box office receipts. One critic was particularly unimpressed with Harlow's role, saying, "In every instance as soon as the producer forgets Helen, the flaxen-haired creature, and takes to the war, his film is absorbing and exciting. But while she is the center of attraction the picture is a most mediocre piece of work. In fact the less said about these glimpses and those in a student's rooms at Oxford the better, for after being filled with admiration for the Zeppelin episode and those dealing with two brothers going forth to bomb a German ammunition dump in an enemy plane, it seems all the more strange that they should have been included in the production."

However, in spite of its slow start, the movie's popularity picked up. People who saw the film liked it, and the best sort of advertising, word of mouth, helped the movie pick up steam. By the end of the year, *Hell's Angels* was the second highest grossing film of 1930. In addition to being her first major film, it would be unique in Harlow's career for another reason. The short scenes shot in color are the only "color pictures" she would ever make.

Chapter 3: A New Star

"I dislike the type of films in which I played that cold, hard type of girl. I haven't even seen two or three of them." – Jean Harlow

While shooting *Hell's Angels*, Harlow met Metro-Goldwyn-Mayer executive Paul Bern. Bern had been born Paul Levy to Jewish parents in Germany, and when he was 9 years old, he and his entire family came to America to escape poverty and anti-Semitism. He grew up in New York City and studied acting at the American Academy of Dramatic Arts. While there, he began using Paul Bern for his stage name and also decided he would rather spend his time behind the camera.

Bern came to Hollywood a few years before Harlow did and tried his hand at directing. By the time the two met, he was employed at MGM as production assistant to Irving Thalberg, and he was also supporting a woman named Dorothy Millette, who considered herself his common law wife and was still living in New York. She had a history of mental illness and required frequent hospitalizations. However, Harlow and Bern hit it off right away, and he became one of her major supporters, encouraging her and guiding her burgeoning career.

Harlow and Bern

Thought he was pleased with her work in *Hell's Angels*, Hughes had no new projects for Harlow to work on once it was finished, so to keep her busy and let the country get to know her better, he sent her on a national tour from Seattle to New York to promote the film. Over the next few months, she would appear at one premier after another, smiling and waving while newspaper reporters snapped her picture. One of the highlights of the trip came when she returned to Kansas City, where she got to see her father and other relatives, not to mention getting to portray herself as the home town girl made good. While she wasn't a big star yet, she certainly seemed to be to folks in the Midwest. That said, Harlow would never grow to enjoy making personal appearances, and though they would continue to be an important of her career, she would never get used to it. One time, she was even heard complaining, "My God, must I always wear a low-cut dress to be important?"

When she returned to Hollywood, Hughes decided to loan her to other studios until he needed her for one of his own pictures again, so she co-starred with Clark Gable in MGM's *The Secret Six*, thanks no doubt to Paul Bern's influence. In remembering the chain of events years later, Harlow would say, "Then, finally, in November, 1930, I got my next chance. I was loaned to Metro-Goldwyn-Mayer for *The Secret Six*. George Hill directed the picture. It was one of the then popular gangster cycle. It marked the first appearance together of the veteran Wallace Beery and the rising newcomer, Clark Gable."

In many ways, Clark Gable would prove to be the most stable male influence in Harlow's life. Though there was never any spark between them, Gable seemed to understand her, both as an actress and a person, and *The Secret Six* was the first of six films Harlow would make with him. She would also make *Iron Man* with Lew Ayres for Universal Studios, but her next big role would be in *The Public Enemy*, starring James Cagney. Released in 1931 by Warner Brothers, *The Public Enemy* tells the story of fictional mobster Tom Powers and his rise through the ranks of organized crime. Harlow played Gwen, a bad woman with a heart of gold and a taste for bad boys. In one of her more memorable scenes, she looks at Cagney and cries, "You are different, Tommy. Very different. And I've discovered it isn't only a difference in manner and outward appearances. It's a difference in basic character. The men I know - and I've known dozens of them - oh, they're so nice, so polished, so considerate. Most women like that type. I guess they're afraid of the other kind. I thought I was too, but you're so strong. You don't give, you take. Oh, Tommy, I could love you to death." Both Harlow and *The Public Enemy* received mixed reviews, but as time went by, appreciation for the film increased, and it is now considered a classic in the gangster movie genre.

Hughes brought Harlow back to his studio to appear in *Platinum Blonde* in 1931, even changing the film's original name (*Gallagher*) to draw attention to her. By this time, Harlow's nearly metallic platinum hair had become a source of fascination for many members of the movie going public. While she always insisted that it was her natural color, there have been rumors through the years that she colored it each week with a combination of ammonia, bleach and soap flakes. This seems unlikely since the combination of ammonia and bleach is a deadly poison, but at the same time, platinum was clearly not her original hair color either. Ever the showman, Hughes promoted "Platinum Blond" clubs throughout the country and even offered a prize of $10,000 to anyone who could recreate the color of Harlow's hair with dyes.

Directed by the famous Frank Capra, *Platinum Blonde* featured Harlow as a spoiled heiress, Anne, married to a down-to-earth reporter. In an unusual turn of events for her pictures, she is the wife who loses her husband to the other woman, instead of the other way around. Except for the fact that it drew more attention to her hair, Harlow's role in this film was unimportant, as was her role in her next movie, *Three Wise Girls*, in 1932.

As it turned out, Harlow's next big splash would be as Daisy in *The Beast of the City*. Again, Bern brokered a deal for MGM to "borrow" her for the picture, and this time, she plays a mob moll willing to do anything for her man, including seducing a young police detective. In scenes that would not be allowed five years later due to the censorship put in place by the Motion Picture Production Code, Harlow is at her most sensual, especially in the following scene when the detective walks in on her stretched across her bed, waiting for him.

"Daisy: I don't mind taking orders, but there's one decision that's always up to me.

Detective: Come on, sit up like a lady! I know that trick!

Daisy: Oh, unintentional, mister.

Daisy: Say, do you think I'm so dumb as to pull a gag like that?

Detective: You might. You're built for it!"

Reflecting on her first year in pictures, Harlow would later say, "Seven pictures in a year, or less? And what pictures! I don't even like to think about them. In all of them I was the same detestable, unsympathetic girl. I determined to leave Hollywood. It was my second goodbye to Hollywood and I believed that I was leaving the screen forever."

Instead, following the movie's release in 1932 Bern took Harlow on yet another theater tour, but this time they focused their attention on East Coast theaters, and this time it was about promoting Harlow personally, not just a movie she was in. The two enjoyed the 10 week tour, and thanks to the packed houses that welcomed her each week, Harlow agreed to extend it for another 6 weeks. That said, it seems Bern had an ulterior motive in planning the tour and making it with her; he was romantically interested in Harlow and wanted a chance to get to know her better. His plan worked, and by the time the two returned to Hollywood in the spring of 1932, they were romantically involved.

Chapter 4: Love and Loss

"Paul, although studious and sometimes inclined to withdraw by himself, loves people and parties. He enjoyed the color and gaiety of crowded rooms and he taught me to share his enjoyment. I went with him to the premiere of 'Hell's Angels,' but I can't ever remember seeing it. I sat through the entire affair in a cold perspiration, trying to realize that the girl on the screen was really me." – Jean Harlow

Growing more infatuated with Harlow every day, Bern went to MGM head Louis B. Mayer and asked him to buy Harlow's contract from Howard Hughes' company, but in spite of Bern's insistence that Harlow would be a valuable asset to the MGM acting pool, Mayer refused. He didn't care what his actresses did in private, but he wanted them to act like ladies in public, and the type of roles that Harlow had been playing repulsed him. After being turned down by Mayer, Bern turned his efforts toward persuading his own boss, Irving Thalberg, to broker a deal with Hughes for Harlow. He convinced him that Harlow had the makings of greatness, and Thalberg agreed to look into the matter. As a result, on her 21st birthday Harlow received the gift of being signed by one of the biggest studios in Hollywood for $1,250 a week. For their part, MGM agreed to pay Hughes $30,000 for the privilege, meaning he made back more than 10 times what he had invested in her over the previous two years.

Thalberg

Harlow's first film under her new contract was the title character in *The Red-Headed Woman*, covering her famous locks with a red wig and starring as a home wrecker who would sleep with any man she needed to in order to get what she wants. Harlow did her first topless scene during this movie while changing her pajama top, and one can only wonder what Bern thought of this, since the two were engaged during the filming and married when it came out. Fortunately, the reviewers were more positive than scandalized. One wrote, "As surprising as the story itself is the appearance in the title role of Jean Harlow, who had never before had a role which imposes so stern a requirement on her acting ability, and she meets the test with flying colors. Those who recall her previous efforts will find a new Jean Harlow in this 'Lil Andrews' of the Katharine Brush tale. In voice and gesture and poise she had gained considerably, doubtlessly through the realization that she plays a role which every actress was said to covet."

However, Harlow had other things on her mind than the picture. She would later remember, "Never will I forget those long happy evenings with Paul after our friendship had matured into love. Then work on *The Red Headed Woman* closed and one evening, while we were discussing matrimony we suddenly decided to be married. I made a personal appearance with the picture on Friday night and on Saturday, July 2, 1932, the ceremony was performed in the living room of my home."

The home in question was a house in Beverly Hills that Bern gave her as a wedding gift. According to one friend, "Paul Bern had no money to speak of and he knew Jean Harlow knew it. Jean Harlow could have married many wealthy men. I think, with that gift, Bern meant to say, 'I haven't anything - but what little I have is yours.'"

Harlow in *Red Dust*

On September 5, 1932, Jean Harlow was on the set of her second picture with Clark Gable, *Red Dust*, when she received word that her husband was dead. Paul Bern had been found that morning on the bathroom floor of their Beverly Hills mansion, shot through the head in what appeared to be a suicide. A note found next to his body appeared to be addressed to Harlow, though she is not mentioned by name. It read,

> "Dearest Dear,
>
> Unfortunately this is the only way to make good the frightful wrong I have done you and to wipe out my abject humiliation, I Love you.
>
> Paul
>
> You understand that last night was only a comedy."

In many ways, the note itself raised more questions than it answered. First, was it indeed written to Harlow? She was not home the previous night but was staying with her mother. She later admitted that the couple had had some sort of argument but would never say what it was about. Also, since they had only been married two months, people wondered what the new bride was doing staying with her mother in the first place. Finally, what had happened the night before? Had she come home and caught him with another woman?

A rumor went around Hollywood, possibly spread by MGM, that Bern was suffering from erectile dysfunction, and that it was the source of his "humiliation." This seems unlikely, since he was still a young man and probably would not call such a thing "a comedy." The next set of questions surrounded the nature of the death itself. While there was of history of mental instability in Bern's family (his mother had committed suicide years earlier), there was, and remains, significant suspicion that Bern was actually murdered. The first possible suspect, and the one the MGM had the most reason to protect, was Harlow, but again, she had little motive. The two had known each other for years and had only been married for two months. What new thing could she have learned about her husband that would drive her to murder? Besides, divorce was not the scandal in Hollywood that it was in the rest of the country. In many ways, it was almost commonplace.

If Bern was murdered, but not by Harlow, then by who? The obvious suspect would be his "wife", Dorothy Millette. She was in California at the time, having come there from New York, she was also known to be violent, and she killed herself two days after Bern's death, jumping from the paddle wheeler *Delta King* and drowning. But then, if Millette killed him, why cover it up? The only valid reason is that, had it become public knowledge that Bern had another wife, he and Harlow would have been branded bigamists. Her career would be over and MGM would have a major stain on its record. It is interesting to note that almost immediately after Bern's death, a move began in the New York legislature to rescind the law recognizing common law marriages. It passed in 1933.

The bottom line is that no one at MGM was nearly as interested in how Bern died as they were in how Harlow would survive. She would later say of that time, "It the midst of my happiness came tragedy. Once again my house of dreams had tumbled about my head. I felt as if my life had ended for me. The only thing that saved me was my work." MGM also made sure that Harlow conducted herself with grace, moving with all the dignity a 21 year old could muster through the September 9, 1932 funeral in Inglewood Park Cemetery. She sat, all in black, through the eulogy by Conrad Nagel and then received the condolences of many of the 2,000 people in attendance. She kept her mouth shut, her head down, and then went back to work.

Chapter 5: Baby Grows Up

"Women like me because I don't look like a girl who would steal a husband. At least not for long." – Jean Harlow

For its part, MGM threw all the corporate weight the studio could muster into protecting Harlow's image. They began releasing information about her early years, referring to her maiden name as "Carpentier" with an "I" to make it sound more stylish. They also mentioned her mother's family and indicated that they were distantly related to the famous writer Edgar Allan Poe. They sent Harlow out to do charity work and then made sure that newspapers were on hand to cover it. The studio clearly wanted its "blonde bombshell" to look like a young widow trying to make it alone in the world.

Unfortunately for MGM, Harlow was not interested in her reputation. Young and smarting from the accusations surrounding Bern's death, she immediately turned her attention and her affections to former boxer Max Baer. The problem was that Baer was still married to actress Dorothy Dunbar, and when Dunbar got wind of the affair, she threatened to file for divorce and name Harlow as a co-respondent for "alienation of affection", thereby accusing her and Baer of adultery. Terrified of another scandal, MGM looked around for some way to distract the public, and they found it by marrying Harlow off to Harold Rosson, a well-known and liked cinematographer from a good family. He was a veteran of World War I and employed at this time by MGM. He and Harlow were friends, and though they were not romantically involved, he was glad to help her out of a jam.

Baer

For a while, it seemed that bad luck would not leave Harlow alone. In mid-October 1933, she was rushed to a hospital with acute appendicitis. She underwent surgery and then spent weeks recovering before she could return to work. Of course, Mother Jean was there around the clock, watching over her "Baby" and barking orders at everyone around her. Rosson remained by her side, playing the dutiful new husband. They would stay married for only a short time until the trouble blew through, but MGM would remember his loyalty by rewarding him with the plum assignment of filming *The Wizard of Oz* a few years later.

Obviously, Harlow had to play along with the ruse the whole time, which she kept up by telling a reporter, "Although the romance ended, our friendship remained. Hal did not fail me. I like him and respect him as much as I did when we were married. It is hard to explain the failure of our match other than to say it simply did not work out as we expected."

Meanwhile, Harlow was still making movies. She was offered the part of Ann Darrow, the giant ape's love interest in *King Kong*, but MGM had already committed her to other projects so she had to turn the role down. As a result, dark haired Fay Wray had to wear a blond wig to play the role, while Harlow made another movie with Clark Gable. In *Hold Your Man*, she is at her wise-cracking best, tossing around one-liners like they were baseballs. One of the best is, "You wouldn't be a bad looking dame, if it wasn't for your face." Never one to take herself too seriously, Harlow later quipped, "They have me singing in a reformatory! My singing would be enough to get me in, but I'd never be able to sing my way out." Audiences loved the movie and Harlow both.

Gable and Harlow in *Hold Your Man*

Perhaps Harlow's most interesting role of 1933 was that of Lola Burns, a sexy film star trying to improve her image by marrying an English noble and adopting a child in the move *Bombshell*. Said to be based at least in part on Harlow's own life (her character also has an overbearing mother and a money-grubbing step-father), the part suited her well, and one even has to wonder how much personal truth she reveals in the following statement: "A glamorous bombshell, eh? A glorified chump, that's what I've been! Well, I'm sick of it, you understand? With the business and everybody! You can get another 'It Girl,' a 'But Girl' or a 'How, When and Where Girl.' I'm clearing out, and you can all stay here in this half-paid-for car barn and get somebody else to pull the apple cart! I'm going where ladies and gentlemen hang their hats and get some peace and quiet... and if any of you try to interfere with me, I'll complain to the authorities!"

After *Bombshell*, Harlow went on to make *Dinner at Eight* with Wallace Berry. In this movie, Harlow played Kitty, the low-class wife of a wealthy man. She and her husband (played by Berry), are invited to a dinner party where she soon learns that her lover is among the guests. One of her best lines in the movie may just be, "Politics? Ha! You couldn't get into politics. You couldn't get in anywhere. You couldn't even get in the men's' room at the Astor!"

1934 proved to be a quiet year for Harlow, as MGM had her make only one picture, *The Girl From Missouri*. Still trying to shape her persona, they gave her the role of Eadie, a young woman running from an unhappy home and trying to survive until she can find a wealthy husband to support her. The critics did not care for Harlow in this type of role, but the public loved her in it and flocked to see the film, making it a box office smash.

Knowing a good thing when they had it, MGM once again cast Harlow to play opposite of Clark Gable in 1935. In *China Seas*, she starred as China Doll, a woman determined to get her man, Captain Alan Gaskell (played by Gable), back. The movie was well made and well received, thanks in large part to the type of rapport built up between the two stars. The following year, Harlow and Gable teamed up again to make *Wife vs. Secretary*. Needless to say, Harlow played the secretary, while sophisticated Myrna Loy played Gable's wife, but this time, Harlow's character is only suspected of being a home wrecker, because she is actually in love with Dave, played by classic good guy Jimmy Stewart. Stewart would later note, "Clarence Brown, the director, wasn't too pleased by the way I did the smooching. He made us repeat the scene about half a dozen times...I botched it up on purpose. That Jean Harlow sure was a good kisser. I realized that until then I had never been really kissed."

Myrna Loy

From 1933-35, Harlow's name always made the "Top Ten Moneymaking Stars Poll" published by the Motion Picture Herald, beginning with a ranking of number 4 in 1933, the highest spot held by any MGM actress. The following year, she dropped to seventh place, but made it back up to the sixth slot in 1935, the same year that she made *Reckless*. This picture would prove to be her first and last musical, which she didn't mind because she knew full well she wasn't a singer. Remembering how she sounded in *Hold Your Man*, she was happy to have singer Virginia Verrill dub in her numbers.

Understandably, MGM had big plans for Harlow by the middle of the decade. Many executives felt that she could step into the shoes left empty by the mysterious Greta Garbo, and at only 23, Harlow could look forward to a long and productive career in movies with her best days in front of her, even as stars like Norma Shearer and Joan Crawford were beginning to see their own primes in the rear view mirror. Ultimately, the motion picture industry was about selling tickets, and that was something Harlow knew how to do. Even as the Great Depression dragged on, people were happy to save their nickels to see the great beauty vamp her way across the screen. In fact, some movie historians believe that it was Harlow's pictures that kept MGM afloat during the time, as other studios around them went bankrupt.

In an interview she gave during this era, Harlow mused:

"The pictures we play have a great deal to do with the traditions that are built up around us. I have done a lot of blond hussies in my day, as well as several in which, as the heroine, I still managed to get into mischief. I am active in my screen roles and it cannot be denied that I am a blond. The combination seems to be fatal.

People who live quiet, unexciting lives like to dream of those who are in the midst of alarms. But if the average girl of my age had to stand the gaff I do in a picture career, she would be ready for the hospital. Not that I don't like it! I do. But one must train for it.

Sex appeal is important. If one had no magnetism, naturally a coldness is apparent on the screen. The response from an audience is likewise cold. The same thing is true in real life. If one is without charm or fascination, beauty wins only half the battle.

There is just enough of mystery and just enough of glamour about picture people to make them interesting to outsiders. But making sequences for film is a tricky business and it is a job. It is hard work and it takes everything we have, but it is worth it."

It was during this time in her life, just after her divorce from Rosson, that Harlow met William Powell, who was in MGM's stable of actors. The two soon fell in love and may have even been planning to marry, but they had some serious differences to work out first. The most important was that Harlow wanted to be a mother, even though she loved her career. She told one of her friends, "I often think that I am missing the very things that make life worth living to these other women who - well, who are kind enough to admire me." Powell, already 42 when they met and the father of a 9 year old boy, was not interested in having a family. The two continued to discuss the issue even as they kept growing closer.

Powell's studio shot in 1936

Harlow was also beginning to enjoy the fortune that came along with her fame. Toward the end of 1935, she told one reporter, "Mother and I are going to Hawaii by boat next month. We will visit a plantation on the island of Oahu and if we like it, I probably will buy it. The China Clipper [airline] service will make it possible to fly there or back in a day, which means I probably would be able to keep up with my studio schedule and still have plenty of time to spend on the plantation." Of course, Harlow knew quite well that she could never move to Hawaii without Mother Jean insisting on moving with her. This was even truer in 1936, because by then, the senior Jean had finally divorced her gold-digging husband.

In addition to *Wife vs. Secretary*, Harlow played the title role in *Suzy* in 1936. Set just before the beginning of World War I, Suzy tells the story of an American showgirl who meets and falls in love with an Irish inventor while living in London. When he is murdered by German spies, she runs away to Paris, where she meets a French flier played by Cary Grant. The two then develop a romance amid the opening salvos of the Great War. However, Harlow was not at her best during the filming, and it showed; *Suzy* became the first of her later films to lose money.

Harlow's next picture, *Riffraff*, was also released in 1936 and also lost money. This time, she starred opposite Spencer Tracy as lovers and employees of a large tuna company. When Tracy's character calls for a strike against management, Harlow's character has to decide who to support, the man she loves or the boss that can give her everything. Of course, true to Hollywood's typical happy ending, she makes the right decision in the end.

Harlow's trailer shot in *Riffraff*

Harlow and Tracy starred together again the same year in *Libeled Lady*. This time Tracy plays newspaperman Warren Haggerty, who persuades his girlfriend Gladys (played by Harlow) to pretend to be married to another man. Needless to say, mayhem ensues, with William Powell playing the man Gladys was falsely married to. This was not what Harlow wanted; she and Powell were together at the time, and she wanted to play his true love, the role Myrna Loy had, so that they could have a great "happily ever after" scene at the end of the movie. However, MGM insisted that this movie remain focused on Powell and Loy. Harlow was part of the wedding scene with Powell, but that wedding on screen would be the only one they'd ever have.

Harlow's trailer shot in *Libeled Lady*

Of course, Harlow didn't know that at the time, and she was still anxiously hoping to remarry again. Perhaps that was the motivation behind her changing her name legally from Harlean Carpenter McGrew Bern Rosson to simply Jean Harlow that year. It was also a good time to make such a change because she was back on top again. *Libeled Lady* earned well over a million dollars for MGM and was even nominated for Best Picture in 1937. Ironically, it lost to The Great Ziegfield, another Powell/Loy movie.

During this time, a reporter came to Harlow's set to interview her. What he found surprised him:

> "The three of us [he, Harlow and Powell] went to her dressing room and, while Jean's hair was being reading for a new sequence, we talked of gambling, Milwaukee beer, dancing, night clubs and most everything else of a common interest. A phonograph blared away with Cab Calloway's music and on occasions Jean would break forth in hi-de-ho song, tap out an 'Off to Buffalo' and crack wise.
>
> Here was the real Jean. The fun loving natural Jean. Her actions confessed her affecting modesty. Here was just an ordinary, everyday happy go lucky, good looking girl imbued with the spirit of life. She was like a devilish school girl

who would let her hair down when the teacher wasn't looking."

Toward the end of 1936, Harlow worked on *Personal Property*, the last film she would complete. In this comedy, directed by W. S. Van Dyke, she plays socialite Crystal Wetherby. Robert Taylor co-starred as a man she hires to watch her home, but she later learns that he has been in prison, leading to the following exchange:

"Crystal Wetherby: And while we're asking so many questions, why were YOU sent to jail?

Raymond Dabney: Murder.

Crystal Wetherby: I wish it had been suicide!"

Chapter 6: Gone Too Soon

"You know, Violet. I have a feeling I'm going away from here and never coming back." – Jean Harlow, speaking to her make-up attendant two weeks before her death.

Following the completion of *Personal Property*, Harlow and the rest of the cast traveled across the country to Washington, D. C. There, on January 30, 1937, they participated in a gala celebration held in honor of President Franklin Roosevelt's 55th birthday, but worn out from filming and the long trip, Harlow came down with influenza while in the frozen city. She seemed to recover completely and was well enough to attend the Academy Award ceremony with Powell on March 4th, and she was supposed to begin filming *Saratoga*, her next picture, just after the ceremony. However, after she had a wisdom tooth pulled a few weeks earlier, it had become badly infected, leading to septicemia. She was treated in a local hospital and then released.

Harlow finally made it to the set on April 22 and filming began, but it was still obvious that she was not well. For one thing, she was nauseous yet also gaining weight. Gable, co-starring with her in what would be their 6th picture together, teased her good naturedly about her weight when he had to lift her during one of their scenes together, but she was tired and retaining water. When she went to her doctor in May, he believed that she had the flu and that her other symptoms, including her abdominal pain, were indicative of a problem with her gall bladder. The problem was that she failed to mention that she'd already had the flu a few months earlier, and that she had gotten a serious sunburn the previous summer.

Though she continued to work, her co-star, Myrna Loy, expressed her concern about how gray her skin looked, and ironically, Harlow was shooting a scene where her character was severely ill when she finally gave up. Leaning against her old friend Gable, she whispered weakly, "I feel terrible. Get me back to my dressing room." Once there, Harlow asked the assistant director to get in touch with Powell, who was nearby filming another picture. Powell rushed over to take her home.

The next day, Powell went in to see how Harlow was and found her sicker than ever. He called a doctor and then contacted Mother Jean, who was on vacation, and told her she needed to come home. Harlow had a history of illness, and at first everyone thought that she was still battling some sort of strain of influenza. By June 3, she was feeling better and sent word to the studio that she would be back on the set the following Monday. That day the Miami News carried a small piece reporting: "Jean Harlow was ill at her home today, believed suffering from inflammation of the gall bladder. Work on her latest picture was suspended. Her physician, Dr. E. C. Fishbaugh, was reported in constant attendance at the bedside of the actress who suffered a severe attack of influenza last February on returning from a personal appearance in Washington."

However, on Sunday afternoon, June 6, she complained to Powell that she was having trouble seeing. He called the doctor again, but Harlow fell into a deep, restless sleep before he arrived. When he did see Harlow, the doctor ordered her to be taken immediately to Good Samaritan Hospital, but within hours, she was in a coma. The next morning, at 11:37 a.m., she was pronounced dead. Jean Harlow was just 26 years old.

According to the hospital records, Harlow had uremia related to kidney failure, and her official cause of death was cerebral edema, a fluid buildup inside the brain caused by kidney failure. Of course, the Hollywood rumor mill would have its say as well. Some claimed that her mother, a Christian Scientist, refused to allow Harlow to be treated, which was patently untrue. Crueler gossips in town speculated that she might have had a venereal disease or even a failed abortion, while the jealous said she must have poisoned by her own hair dye. In reality, chances are the seeds for Harlow's death were planted back when scarlet fever weakened her kidneys. The infections from her tooth extraction, as well as her case of influenza, only made matters worse. Though she was a young woman, she did live a fast life, and her heavy drinking and stressful environment may have led to high blood pressure, another cause of kidney failure.

Regardless of why it happened, Harlow's death stunned Hollywood. She was so young and vibrant that nobody could believe she was actually gone. MGM closed on June 9, the day of her funeral, and one man wrote, "The day Baby died there wasn't one sound in the commissary for three hours." Those who attended the simple service held at the Forest Lawn Memorial Park in Glendale saw Jean in her coffin wearing the beautiful gown she had last worn when filming *Libeled Lady*. Her hands held a white gardenia and a note from William Powell saying, "Goodnight, my dearest darling." Following the service, Harlow was interred in a private room in the Cemetery's Great Mausoleum, and her inscription simply read, "Our Baby." Mother Jean would join her there 21 years later.

At first, MGM thought it would be best to shoot *Saratoga* again with another actress, but the public was curious about Harlow's last role, so they managed to complete it using doubles and re-written scenes. Released about a month after Harlow's death, it became MGM second highest grossing film of the year.

In addition to her films, Harlow left behind another gift for her fans. Sometime around 1934 or 35, she wrote a novel entitled *Today is Tonight*. Upon her death, Mother Jean passed the rights to make the book into a movie to MGM, but she kept the rights to publish the book for herself. Through the years, she apparently forgot about those publishing rights, and when the rights passed to a family friend in 1958, she sold the rights to Grove Press, who published it in hardcover in 1965. Mademoiselle magazine ran a syndicated version of the book that same year, with the disclaimer that "it had been presented not for its literary quality, but as a simple, revealing commentary on the flamboyant Twenties and the sobering Thirties by an idol of the era."

Set in the early 1930s, *Today is Tonight* tells that story of a wealthy society couple suffering through physical and financial ruin after the stock market crash of 1929. As is often the case with first time authors, Harlow likely wrote it to create on paper the kind of life she wanted to have in reality. Sadly, *Today is Tonight* would be the closest she ever got to a happy ending.

Carole Lombard

Chapter 1: Play Fair

"You'll find that men usually play fair. It's all very well to say that you want to back out of a bargain because you've changed your mind. That's supposed to be a woman's privilege. But men don't play the game that way. A man who says he'll do a thing and then reneges, is soon put where he belongs, out in the cold. If I say I'll do something, I make it stick." – Carole Lombard

At one point during the height of her career, Carole Lombard was asked by a reporter about her "rules for living". While she had no answer for him at that moment, she decided to give the matter some thought and eventually came up with what she referred to as her "golden rules". These 10 rules both shaped the way she lived and were shaped by her life.

Carole Lombard learned to "play fair" on the streets of a cozy little upper-middle-class neighborhood in Fort Wayne, Indiana, where she was born on October 6, 1908, and named Jane Alice Peters by her parents. Her father, Frederic Peters, was from one of the best families in Fort Wayne, as was her mother, Elizabeth Knight Peters, whom the family called Bessie. Bessie's father, Charles Knight, held extensive interests in banks along the East Coast of the United States, and when his daughter married Frederic, he used his influence to get his new son-in-law a cushy position with the Horton Company, a local washing machine manufacturer. Washing machines were new technology at the turn of the 20th century, and Frederic Peters' career grew as their popularity spread across Indiana.

Little Jane Alice was her parents' third child, and only daughter, joining Frederic Peters Junior

(1902) and Stuart (1906). With two brothers as her primary playmates, Jane Alice soon became something of a tomboy, enjoying running through the neighborhood with her brothers more than sitting quietly with the book, and her rambunctious antics helped her develop a body that was well-suited for physical comedy. Indeed, she would later build her career around "screwball antics".

The one thing that could get Little Jane Alice to sit still was a chance to watch a movie. In Fort Wayne, Indiana during the years leading up to World War I, Friday night was movie night down at the Colonial Theatre. But while other little girls might have been attracted to storybook tales of love and dramas of princes and princesses, little Jane Alice preferred action features. Furthermore, she enjoyed acting out what she'd seen on the screen, leading one friend to remember that "Friday's movie outing dictated Saturday's play activities." It was fortunate for both Jane Alice and her future audiences that her mother had once wanted to be an actress, because it was unusual for middle-class people in Fort Wayne to patronize what many considered to be a "lower class" form of entertainment like films. Bessie was comfortable enough with her position in the community not to care what other people said, so she and Jane Alice often spent Friday evenings in front of the dancing black and white images scattered across the theater screen.

There was another reason why Jane Alice was so much more inclined to copy the movement on screen rather than the lines: she grew up in the era of silent movies. Jane Alice's impressions of acting were formed in a time when actresses only mouthed the words on screen, and where all the action was accompanied by live music played in the theater during the performance. Therefore, while Lombard's movements were learned from others, her voice, and her way of speaking, would be all her own.

As a tomboy in a neighborhood full of boys, Jane Alice naturally learned the virtues of being good at sports. She was athletic by nature and was nearly as good as her brothers at all sports, from baseball to swimming. She mastered the latter during family summers spent on Sylvan Lake in Rome City, Indiana; like many upper-middle-class families of that era, the Peters made it a practice to take a cottage on the lake during the summer to get away from the heat and humidity of the city.

During her early years, Jane Alice's life was mostly uneventful, but in 1913 a flood struck Fort Wayne that would stand out in the memory of every person living there at that time. The Peters home, located on a hill above the St. Mary's River, was spared from flooding but quickly became a staging ground for volunteers trying to stave off the river's waters. It also helped that the Peters family had one of the few telephones in the area, so Jane Alice watched with fascination as her mother coordinated the efforts of both those fighting the flood and those supporting the flood fighters. Bessie also managed to be a model mother by successfully keeping her children from being frightened, something she accomplished by making them her assistants.

In the year following the Fort Wayne flood, the Peters family suffered a tragedy on a much more personal scale. Frederic Peters had been injured the year before his marriage in an industrial accident, and while the most obvious result of the accident was a severe leg injury that left him with a limp the rest of his life, he also suffered some sort of traumatic brain injury that left him with severe mood swings and headaches. As the years wore on, these mood swings came to have more and more of detrimental effect on his marriage and family life. Things finally came to a head in 1914 when Bessie decided to take an "extended vacation" to California. Removing her children from the local public school, she packed them up, along with all their clothes, for the "trip". Neither she nor the children would ever return to their home in Fort Wayne, and Bessie later referred to this move as a "Victorian divorce," in which a husband and wife agreed to remain married but live apart.

Chapter 2: Don't Brag

"Men can brag, but that's where a woman can't do what men do, and still be feminine. No man will endure listening to a girl boast about how smart she is." – Carole Lombard

Jane Alice's teen years certainly gave her little to brag about. Though her father continued to send his wife and children money even after they moved to California, the kids and their mom were no longer able to live the kind of lifestyle they had enjoyed in Indiana. On top of that, there was the inherent stigma of being the child of a broken home, a very prevalent issue in early 20th century America. Bessie quickly learned that while her maiden name gave her a certain status in Fort Wayne, she was just another ex-wife in Los Angeles.

Little is known about what six-year-old Jane Alice thought of leaving her home and her father because she would never speak of it publicly herself, but some critics and biographers have concluded that this early family tragedy gave her acting, even her comedic acting, a tragic edge that made it more appealing. And naturally, the move to Los Angeles improved her chances of being discovered, which occurred while she was only 12 years old and caught up in a baseball game with her brothers and their friends along the quiet streets of the residential part of the city. Up until that time, Jane Alice had expressed no interest in acting and was simply an average student at Virgil Mary Middle School looking forward to a "normal" life as a teenager, but director Alan Dwan would change that. He later recalled the first time he saw her, saying Jane Alice was "out there knocking the hell out of the other kids, playing better baseball than they were. And I needed someone of her type for this picture." In an event that most children could only dream of, he approached Jane Alice, and then Bessie, and got their permission to test the girl for the role of main character Monte Blue's little sister in the 1921 film *A Perfect Crime*.

Alan Dwan

Young Jane Alice in *A Perfect Crime* **(1921)**

For her part, Jane Alice initially seemed to take the whole experience in stride; after two days on set shooting her part, she returned to Virgil Mary Middle School, finished her studies there, and moved on to Fairfax High School. However, she had indeed been bitten by the acting bug and continued to go on auditions. Her next big break came in the spring of 1924, when she was crowned the "May Queen" at Fairfax, because one of the men attending the school carnival was a talent scout for Charlie Chaplin. He spotted Jane Alice on the stage and approached her about appearing in Chaplin's next film, *The Gold Rush*. Even when her screen test for this movie did not go well and she did not receive the part, the offer did open up other professional opportunities for the 15-year-old girl. A representative of the Pictogram Film Company saw her screen test and approached her about signing a movie contract with them. Once again, she was never given the contract, but in conversations with the studio representative, she learned that he considered her name too boring for an actress and suggested that she change it. Remembering a girlfriend that she often played tennis with in middle school, she subsequently chose Carol as her screen name.

Despite still being a teenager, Carol Peters continued to look for work as an actress, and in October 1924, she received a contract with the Fox Film Corporation. While it is unclear exactly how she came to the attention of studio head Winfield Sheehan, it seems likely that Bessie contacted Hollywood gossip columnist Louella Parsons on her daughter's behalf. Parsons in turn got Carol a screen test and an invitation to a dinner party where she knew a number of studio bigwigs would be present. One or both of these events attracted Sheehan's attention, and he offered her a contract as an actress for the princely sum of $75 per week. Not surprisingly, once that offer was on the table, Carol left high school with her mother's blessing, but she was able to graduate by special arrangement in 1927.

Louella Parsons

Carol Peters had to make one more name change as part of her new life. While Fox thought that Carol was an excellent first name for an actress, they weren't so happy with Peters. Again thinking of a family friend, Carol suggested the new surname of Lombard. Fox agreed, and thus high school student Jane Alice Peters had become Carol Lombard.

Although Lombard would come to be one of the most popular actresses in Hollywood within just a few years, her first few appearances on the screen were spent playing small roles in B-grade Westerns and adventure dramas. Later, when Lombard had the career security to complain, she remembered, "All I had to do was simper prettily at the hero and scream with terror when he battled with the villain." Still, she was in many ways a small-town girl in the big city, and she enjoyed the more glamorous aspects of moviemaking, including socializing with actors on the set and showing up for costume fittings and photo shoots. The 1920s was very beginning of Hollywood's heyday, and the perfect setting for a carefree girl in her teens. Lombard soon became a well-known flapper and a fixture in all the best nightclubs whose dancing at the Coconut Grove even won her several prizes in the Charleston category.

Finally, in the spring of 1925, Lombard scored her first leading role opposite Edmond Lowe in *Marriage in Transit*, a film that did a good job of highlighting her best acting skills, and the critics liked her. In spite of her success in this movie, however, Fox came to the conclusion that she was not the actress they needed in their stable at that time, so the studio decided not to renew her one-year contract. Part of the problem had come about because of an accident earlier in 1925 when Lombard suffered a freak injury when the car in front of hers rolled backwards and hit her car. While she was not seriously injured, she did suffer a nasty cut on the left side of her face. The cut healed well, but it still left a scar that some critics feel led Fox to cut her.

Teenage plastic surgery is controversial even today, and in 1925 it was nearly unheard of, but nevertheless, Carol sought out the best plastic surgeon in Hollywood and convinced him to repair the scar. While it was still slightly noticeable, for the rest of her career she was able to cover it with makeup and disguise it with careful lighting. As far as anyone could tell, it never bothered her again.

Chapter 3: Obey the Boss

"A career girl who competes with men has to learn that rule — or else. If she won't accept discipline, or bow to the rules of the institution and take orders, she can't succeed. I know that the picture director knows best. I remember when I was making 'My Man Godfrey' with William Powell. Gregory La Cava was directing. One day he was ill, but he insisted that work go on while he rested. 'You know what to do,' he told us. 'Just pretend I'm there and go ahead.' Well, it didn't work. Bill and I were used to taking orders because it's part of the discipline of the studio. It was a simple scene, we knew what to do, but the director wasn't there and we felt lost. Somebody has to be the boss in every big enterprise, and if the boss is absent the business soon comes to a halt." – Carole Lombard

For the next year, Carole Lombard searched for work around Hollywood but found none, and it began to seem as though her early career was just a flash in the pan. Fortunately, she was still just 18 years old and too young to realize that she could fail, so she continued to try out for every part she thought she might be suitable for. She also visited studios looking for jobs, and her tenacity paid off when she was offered a position as a Sennett Bathing Beauty. This happened when she decided to take a chance and try comedic acting by doing a screen test for Mack Sennett, who was known as the "King of Comedy" in Hollywood. At first, Lombard felt that slapstick comedy was both beyond her reach and beneath her dignity as an actress, but she soon discovered that she had a real talent for that style of comedy. Over the next 18 months, between

September 1927 and March 1929, Lombard made 15 short films for Sennett. Not only did this give her valuable exposure to the American public, it also gave Lombard her first experience in comedy. She found that she liked making people laugh, and over a decade later, she would refer to her time working for Sennett as "the turning part of my acting career." Ironically, she was occasionally credited as Carole Lombard in the Sennett films, even though she would not legally add the "e" until 1936, suggesting those early credits were merely mistakes.

Mack Sennett

Carol Lombard in *Run, Girl, Run* (1928)

About a year into her work for Sennett, his company, Pathe Exchange, began casting Lombard in full-length pictures, and after playing a bit role in the film *Power*, she landed the part of Blonde Rosie in *Me Gangster*. This led to a larger role in the film *Show Folks*, in which she played a gold-digging vaudevillian actress named Cleo. She did well enough in that performance to ensure she was subsequently cast as Ginny in *Ned McCobb's Daughter*.

All of her good work in these roles led to her first "big break" in *High-Voltage*. In that film, which was also her first "talkie", she played a young woman stranded with a group of diverse people during a snowstorm. While *High-Voltage* cast her in a dramatic role, her next film, *Big News*, was a comedy. She played opposite Robert Armstrong and received excellent reviews for her work, and the public also found her attractive, making it obvious that she had a real talent for comedy. Lombard would go on to act opposite Armstrong again in *The Racketeer* in 1929, and a critic wrote about that film, "Carol Lombard proves a real surprise, and does her best work to date. In fact this is the first opportunity she has had to prove that she has the stuff to go over."

That critic wasn't the only one beginning to think that way. In 1930, Fox, thinking that they might have made a mistake in initially letting Lombard go, cast her in *The Arizona Kid*. They were taking something of a chance, since they were counting on the movie being a blockbuster and had cast one of their biggest stars, Warner Baxter, in it. Clearly, they must have seen something in the aspiring actress or they would not have given Lombard third billing. The film lived up to their expectations, and Lombard was once more praised by both the critics and the viewing public, but Fox executives still did not sign her to a contract, a decision that they would soon come to regret.

Lombard and Baxter in *The Arizona Kid*

When Fox balked, Paramount recruited and ultimately hired Lombard, giving her a contract for $350 dollars a week. They wasted little time putting her to work either, quickly casting her opposite Buddy Rogers in *Safety in Numbers*. Of Lombard's work in this comedy, one critic raved that Lombard "proves an ace comedienne." Interestingly, when she starred with Miriam Hopkins in *Fast and Loose*, Paramount Studio executives mistakenly had Carol's name spelled with an "e" in the credits, just like in some of the Sennett films. Lombard was assured that it would be corrected in future films, but she decided that she liked the way it looked on screen. From that point forward, she would be credited as Carole Lombard, even though the official name change didn't come for several more years. When she heard reports that she had added the "e" to the end of Carol because she was a numerologist, Lombard replied, "That's a lot of bunk."

In 1931, Lombard learned firsthand just how hard the life of an actress of that era could be, as she had to make five films that year. In the first, the comedy *It Pays to Advertise*, she played Mary Grayson, a young secretary caught up in a hilarious scheme with the boss's son. Then she starred opposite of Paramount's premiere leading man, William Powell, in her next two films. In both *Man Of The World* and *Ladies Man*, she played an innocent young woman caught up in farcical situations that she did not understand. There was good chemistry between her and Powell both on and off screen, as future events would demonstrate.

In her next film, *Up Pops the Devil*, Lombard tried for a slightly more sophisticated role by playing Mary, the wife of a struggling writer who takes a job as a Broadway dancer to support him while he writes. Lombard played another young wife in her final film of 1931, *I Take This Woman*, in which she starred as Kay Dowling, the city-slicker wife of Gary Cooper's cowboy character. Unable to give up her "big city ways," she plans to divorce him, but as was typical of the movies of that era, she realized that she was still in love with her husband and did not want a divorce. In the end, as always, they all lived happily ever after.

Chapter 4: Take Criticism

"Men have learned to take criticism, that is, the successful men. The ones who flare up and go home mad are the kind who never get the last installment paid on the radio. Here again the movies have taught me. I have learned to take criticism and stand up to it like a man. Yet a woman will simply burn if you hint that the hat she's got on doesn't look quite perfect, or that she might, just might, have led from the queen, jack, ten instead of tossing in an eight spot. I went to a showing of the first rough cut of 'Swing High, Swing Low,' in a small college town. In the tragic scene, where I screwed up my face to cry (I can't help it if I look that way when I cry), the audience laughed. When I really turned it on and emoted, they howled. It was heartbreaking. I felt like crawling under the seats and losing myself among the gum and other useless things. But I had to take it. If you're playing according to masculine rules, which is required of any girl with a career, you've got to accept criticism and profit by it. Otherwise how could you become a singer, decorator, painter or private secretary? I learned something from that experience, too. I'm best if I top off tears with a laugh. A star who is too big for criticism sooner or later loses out. That goes for working women, too." – Carole Lombard

Lombard certainly had plenty of opportunities to learn how to take criticism during her early career. Though she was working hard and had received praise for various roles, she was not making the impact on the critics or the American public that she hoped to make in 1931. Lombard kept at it by making five more movies in 1932. The first two, *No Man's Land* and *Sinners in the Sun*, were both critical and box office failures, but her third film, *Virtue*, did better. In that film, she played a fast talking New York girl named Mae opposite of Pat O'Brien, who played Jimmy Doyle, a cabbie whom she first stiffed and then fell in love with. The two romped through the movie, getting into and out of every kind of trouble, before finally finding their happy ending.

Lombard returned to drama in her fourth film of that year, *No More Orchids*, this time playing a spoiled heiress named Annie Holt who is forced into an arranged marriage in order to save her father's bank. In her fifth and final film, *No Man of Her Own*, Lombard played for the first and last time opposite Clark Gable. As librarian Connie Randall, she made a strange counterpart to Gable's con man character, Babe Stewart, and though the two shared several passionate love scenes together, Lombard later recalled that there was no spark between her and Gable. She once said of her future husband that they "did all kinds of hot love scenes ... and I never got any kind of tremble out of him at all." Nevertheless, the critics liked the picture, with one calling it "arguably Carole Lombard's best performance to date."

Lombard again tried her hand at drama in 1933 in *From Hell to Heaven*, in which she played Colly Tanner, a woman desperate to win a bet she had placed on a horse race, and she followed this performance with her only role in a horror film, the poorly received *Supernatural*. Then came *The Eagle and the Hawk*, where her character was only known by the mysterious name of "The Beautiful Lady." In *Brief Moment*, Lombard played Abby Fane, a nightclub singer married to a wealthy playboy, and she played another nightclub singer in *White Woman*, this time opposite of Charles Laughton. Laughton played Horace Prin, Lombard's insanely jealous and cruel husband.

Lombard was making a lot of movies, but as the disparate roles suggested, Paramount didn't seem to know quite what to do with her. She didn't have to worry about being typecast, but she also hadn't established a niche either.

Chapter 5: Love is Private

"When it comes to your personal life, such as love and romance, girls should take a tip from the men and keep their affairs to themselves. Any man worth his salt regards his private life as his own. To kiss a girl and run and tell would mark him as a cad. Why doesn't that apply to girls also?" – Carole Lombard

In 1931, Lombard fell in love with and married her costar, William Powell. At that time, Powell was Paramount's best-selling actor, and Lombard often mentioned that she had been a fan of his before they ever met, one time saying, "Bill Powell is the only intelligent actor I've ever met." Many people questioned what they saw in each other; after all, the 22 year old was 16 years his junior and had a reputation for being something of a loose cannon given to vulgar language and wild behavior, whereas Powell was known as the quiet, intellectual type. Lombard was well aware of these differences herself, and she insisted that the "love between two people who are diametrically different" was a "perfect see-saw love".

Powell was more philosophical, telling a reporter:

"We open secret doors in one another's personalities. We've found that we are new people to each other. Carole is supposed to be the sophisticated type. I'm supposed to be suave and polished – I'm supposed to drip with polish and slide with suavity. Well, it isn't true. We are both the shyest, most sensitive people you'll ever know. Carole's supposed sophistication is just a mask she has used to get over the hard bumps of life. Nobody knows where I got my reputation for suaveness. After our honeymoon we're going to settle down in the old-fashioned idea of a calm and very unexciting life-as exciting lives are judged in Hollywood. We have a few close friends who mean much to us. We're going to play tennis and quietly attend theaters-other than opening nights-and take drives to the beaches and get our own meals on the cook's day out and go places and do things-always together. I've found a pal, a sweetheart, a friend, a wife…"

Ultimately, the marriage between the two proved not to be a "perfect seesaw", and they divorced just over two years after they married. Though she initially blamed their careers for getting in the way, Lombard later admitted to a reporter that their work "had little to do with the divorce. We were just two completely incompatible people." In spite of their incompatibility, Lombard and Powell would remain friends for the rest of her life, and she even gave him credit for helping her get the part in *My Man Godfrey* that earned her the only Oscar nomination of her career.

Lombard and Powell in *My Man Godfrey*

Lombard would later wonder if she was actually cut out for the role of a wife, telling one reporter "I think marriage is dangerous. The idea of two people trying to possess each other is wrong. I don't think the flare of love lasts. Your mind rather than your emotions must answer for the success of matrimony. It must be a friendship- a calm companionship which can last through the years." However, she apparently changed her mind a few years later, because in 1936, she again found herself involved with a former leading man. This time, it was the dashing Clark Gable, then considered to be one of the most handsome men in America. The two started dating in 1936 and soon fell in love.

Wanting to "make an honest woman out of" Lombard, Gable approached his wife, Ria Langham, for a divorce, but even though they had been separated for some time, and well before Gable had started dating Lombard, Langham at first refused to grant the divorce. As time went on, however, Gable and Lombard became more serious about each other, and Langham soon realized that her husband would not be returning to her. She agreed to grant him a divorce in return for a settlement of $500,000. Their divorce became final in March 1939, and Gable and Lombard quickly headed Kingman, Arizona, where they married on the 29th of that month.

Throughout their short marriage, Lombard would maintain a strange balance between near reverence for her husband and crass, cutting remarks about the most intimate parts of their lives. On the one hand, she once told a reporter who asked about her efforts to balance her work and her marriage, "Pa comes first." (Pa was her pet name for Gable, and he called her "Ma.") On the other hand, she also told another reporter, "God knows I love Clark, but he's the worst lay in the town." For his part, perhaps because he was a man, or perhaps because he considered talking badly about his wife to be tacky, Gable was more taciturn in his comments about Lombard. When a reporter asked him about their life together, he once replied simply, "With her, it was like music, it was completely natural."

Gable and Lombard in 1939

Chapter 6: Work - And Like It!

"All women should have something worthwhile to do, and cultivate efficiency at it, whether it's housekeeping or raising chickens. Working women are interesting women. And they're easier to live with. Idle women who can think of nothing to do with their time are dangerous to themselves and to others. The only 'catty' women I've known were idlers, with nothing to do but gossip and make trouble. A woman has just as much right in this world as a man and can get along in it just as well if she puts her mind to it. Take business-that's supposed to be a man's province. Yet I can name you the most outstanding success in the business life of the movies and that person is a woman: Mary Pickford. You can't match her. She's supreme in every department. As a matter of fact, women have an advantage in business. Men are so secure in their belief that they are supreme in business that they are often caught napping by alert women. Man thinks he's dealing with an inferior brain when it comes to woman, and that makes him a sucker. Furthermore, women have a highly developed sense of intuition that's just as valuable as hardheaded logic." – Carole Lombard

1934 proved to be both Lombard's hardest working and most successful year as an actress. It began with the release of *Bolero*, in which she once again played a nightclub dancer, this time opposite George Raft. In order to accept her role in Bolero, Lombard had turned down the opportunity to star again opposite of Gable in *It Happened One Night*, probably due at least in part to her perceived lack of chemistry with Gable the first time they acted together. She would not start dating Gable for a few more years.

While she may have regretted the decision later, Lombard was happy enough to get to showcase some of her dancing skills with the graceful Raft. The movie did well and opened the doors for her to make her next film, *We're Not Dressing*. In *We're Not Dressing*, a musical comedy, Lombard played Doris Worthington, a socialite stranded on an island with a hilarious mix of people, all played by some of the biggest musical and comedic stars of that era. Not only did Lombard star in the film, she played opposite Bing Crosby, George Burns, Gracie Allen, and the legendary Ethel Merman. Not surprisingly, the film was a major hit with audiences and critics alike, and 30 years later, this film would prove to be the inspiration for the television series "Gilligan's Island".

It was a happy stroke of nepotism that won Lombard one of her most famous roles. Her second cousin, the director Howard Hawks, ran into Lombard at a party. He later recalled that she was quite drunk, but he found her behavior "hilarious and uninhibited and just what the part needed" for his new film, *Twentieth Century*. It would be this movie that finally earned Lombard the star power and recognition she had been looking for. Lombard was cast as diva Lily Garland, who had been born Mildred Plotka and been in love with a fellow Broadway actor, John Barrymore's Oscar Jaffe. While Garland's star had risen and she was now working in Hollywood, Jaffe's career had tanked, and he hoped to lure his former girlfriend back on stage for one more career saving show.

A lobby card for the film

At first, it seemed that Hawks might have made a mistake in casting Lombard in the role, because she was having trouble conforming her acting to the role. However, he continued to work with her, encouraging her to loosen up and play the role the way she felt it should be played. His coaching worked, and Barrymore later called Lombard "the finest actress I have worked with, bar none." For her own part, Lombard could not believe the change that came over her during the filming. She told one reporter, "In the rushes of *Twentieth Century* that I have seen, I hardly recognize myself. I certainly am not the Carole Lombard of the past four years."

She was not the only one who noticed the change. One critic said of her performance, "Lombard is like no other Lombard you've seen before. When you see her, you'll forget the rather stilted Lombard of old. You'll see a star blaze out of this scene, high spots Carole never dreamed of hitting." Another critic raved that "she vibrates with life and passion, abandon and diablerie". Depression-era audiences, desperate for movies that made them laugh, loved *Twentieth Century* and made it a hit. *Twentieth Century* also marked the first of what would come to be known as "screwball comedies", and Carole Lombard would be this new genre's first Queen.

Lombard either never heard of or chose to ignore W.C. Fields' advice to "never work with dogs or children", because in her next film, entitled *Now and Forever*, she starred opposite a pretty little actress with golden curls named Shirley Temple. In the film, Lombard played Toni Day, a wealthy socialite looking for something to give her life meaning, and she finds it in Temple's Penny, an orphan girl needing a home. As always, Temple's character worked her dimpled magic on both Day and her husband, and the three formed a family destined to last "now and forever."

Lombard played a completely different type of character in *A Lady by Choice*. In this film, her character, Alabam Lee, is a professional fan dancer trying to shore up her reputation. To do so, she "adopts" an elderly woman whom she hopes will provide her with a suitable "mother figure" to introduce to the press. Instead, the woman, Patsy Patterson, turns out to be an alcoholic street lady. However, it is through Patsy that Alabam meets Johnny Mills, a goodhearted lawyer. The two fall in love and, in spite of interference from several sources, marry in the end.

In the last of the six movies Lombard made in 1934, *The Gay Bride*, she plays a gangster's moll. This film, in which she starred with Chester Morris, was clearly a departure from her most recent movies' roles and was panned by both the critics and movie audiences. Lombard made one more dance picture with George Raft, *Rumba*, which was released in 1935 to mixed reviews.

If it wasn't clear after *Twentieth Century*, the last few movies of 1934 led Lombard to realize that her true talent lay in making people laugh.

Chapter 7: The Cardinal Virtue is a Sense of Humor

"Do you laugh in the right places? Then, you'll get along, in fair weather or foul. Humor is nothing less than a sense of the fitness of things. Something that's out of proportion, like an inflated ego, should strike you funny, particularly if it's your own inflated ego. Otherwise you are pathetic and quite hopeless." – Carole Lombard

Many have been amazed both by Lombard's comedic timing and that such a beautiful woman would choose to play the ditzy blond so often. However, Desi Arnaz, himself no stranger to either women or comedy, once noted how well the two worked together: "Carole had a quality which is rare. You can count the women who have had it on the fingers of one hand. Carole, while doing the wild antics of a clown...could make you laugh, and yet at the same time make you want to go to bed with her." One of her favorite directors, Mitchell Leisen, agreed, remembering, "We called her 'The Profane Angel' because she looked like an angel but she swore like a sailor. She was the only woman I ever knew who could tell a dirty story without losing her femininity."

Lombard would go on to make her second "screwball" comedy in 1935. Titled *Hands Across the Table*, it told the story of a poor manicurist trying to snag a wealthy husband. Lombard played opposite Hollywood newcomer Fred MacMurray, and remembering the help she had received earlier in her career, Lombard went out of her way to work with him and teach him the fine art of comedy. The two worked well together, and the film was such a success that the two became a new Hollywood feature, starring together in three more films.

Lombard and MacMurray in *Hands Across the Table*

In 1936, Lombard filmed a new project called *Love Before Breakfast*, which one critic characterized as "*The Taming of the Shrew*, screwball style". This film did not do very well, but that did not deter Lombard, who had found her acting style and her most affective genre. She returned again to working with MacMurray in *The Princess Comes Across*, playing an actress who hopes to win a film contract by pretending to be a Swedish princess. Many in Hollywood considered the movie to be a satiric look at the life and career of Greta Garbo, but regardless, the critics loved it and audiences found it hilarious. Garbo was known as being something of a diva, but no one would accuse Lombard of having that problem. She enjoyed making fun of herself as much a she did anyone else, one time telling a reporter, "You ought to see the map for my face in the Makeup Department. It looks like a landscape of the moon."

Although they had divorced just a few years earlier, Lombard teamed up with ex-husband William Powell in *My Man Godfrey* in 1935. Universal Studios wanted Powell for the part of Godfrey, and he refused to play it unless they cast Lombard as his female lead. He believed that she was just the one to play Irene, an heiress who, believing Powell's character to be homeless, hires him as her family's butler. Unbeknownst to her, Godfrey is actually a millionaire himself. Director Gregory LaCava was an old friend of Lombard's and knew her well, so instead of giving her very specific directions, he instructed her to draw on her own "eccentric nature." Sensing that this role could be her best ever, Lombard worked especially hard on her part, paying close attention to make sure that every expression of Irene was just right.

Her hard work paid off, and *My Man Godfrey* opened to loud applause from both the audience in the theater and the critics in the papers. The new movie was nominated for six Academy Awards, with Lombard garnering her first and only nomination for Best Actress. Many critics today still feel that it was her finest performance, and the film established her position as one of Hollywood's most important actresses.

In 1936, Lombard returned to working with MacMurray in *Swing High Swing Low*, which was a drama that gave Lombard and MacMurray both several chances to showcase their comedic timing. The two play star-crossed cabaret performers trying to maintain a relationship and careers at the same time. Though *Swing High Swing Low* did well among viewers, Lombard did not enjoy working on the drama as much as she had previous comedies. She was scouting around for a new picture to throw herself into when she learned that David O. Selznick had hired Hollywood screenwriter Ben Hecht to create a role specifically for her in the new movie *Nothing Sacred*. This film teamed Lombard up with Fredric March and was a satiric look at journalism and journalists, with Lombard starring as a small-town girl who feigns her own fatal illness in order to get attention. Her story is picked up by a New York reporter, played by March, and after that things get seriously out of hand. The film was directed by William Wellman and was the only color picture Lombard ever made, and it was personally one of Lombard's favorite films of her career.

Lombard in *Nothing Sacred*

In 1937, Lombard starred in what was arguably her funniest movie, *True Confessions*, which paired her one last time with both John Barrymore and Fred MacMurray. In it she and MacMurray play the ultimate odd couple; he is an honest, hardworking and failing lawyer, while she is a compulsive liar who cannot stay out of trouble. Things get out of hand when she takes a new job with a man who ends up dead, and the police charge her with the crime despite her claims she did not commit it. Her husband agrees to defend her despite believing she is guilty, and laughter ensues as this version of the "boy who cried wolf" plays out. Their problems do not end even when she is acquitted, as John Barrymore's character attempts to blackmail them.

The first time she read the script, Lombard predicted the film "smacked of a surefire success", and she was proven right when True Confessions opened to rave reviews and packed theatres. In fact, the film was so popular that Lombard's agent, David Selznick's famous brother Myron, negotiated a new deal for her with Paramount. Her new salary would total $450,000 per year, more than four times what President Franklin Roosevelt was making, and when the press questioned her about her high salary, she reminded them that 80% would go to taxes. She then shocked everyone by adding that she didn't mind paying taxes because "Every cent anybody pays in tax is spent to benefit him. There's no better place to spend it. I enjoy this country and I really think I get my money's worth." Lombard's words reached the ears of President Roosevelt himself, who wrote her a personal note thanking her for her kind support and patriotism.

The lobby card for the movie

In spite of her raise from Paramount, Lombard still left the company in 1938, and that year she made one of the worst films of her career, *Fools of Scandal*, for Warner Brothers. It was supposed to be a comedy about a wealthy actress (Lombard) who, while visiting Paris, meets a down-on-his luck chef. When she returns to London, he follows her and takes a job in her home, but when her fiancé discovers that she has a man living in her house, he objects, leading to tension between the three and a classic love triangle. This time, both the script and the chemistry between the actors was not up to par, and the film was a bomb. One of the reasons for its failure may have been that Lombard's heart was not in her work at that time. She and Gable had just married, and she was no longer as interested in working as she had been. From 1925-1934, she had made an average of six movies a year, and after 1935, that number dropped to an average of two films per year.

Obviously, there were other factors playing into Lombard's decision to make fewer movies. As a huge star, she could now afford to be pickier about the roles she chose, and she could also afford not to work as hard.

Chapter 8: Be Consistent

Lombard once explained one of the most important qualities an actress needed to have a successful career:

> "By that, I mean you should take a hint from the men. They are terribly consistent, as a rule. You can tell what they'll do in any given circumstance. If a girl puts her best foot forward at the office, she shouldn't change steps when she gets home. A career girl must be neatly turned out, even-tempered and willing to take orders at work, and there's no reason why she must check these virtues with her hat and coat when she leaves her place of business. I manage to add enough inconsistency to my behavior at the studio so that I'm the same there as at home; inclined to blow off steam at odd moments or be very demure and sweet-tempered — just to keep 'em guessing. In fact I've got myself guessing. I don't quite know which way I am. That's being consistently inconsistent, anyway.

> Men are about the same at home as they are at work. Don't say it's because they lack the imagination to be otherwise — just take the hint. Men are creatures of habit and comfort, and they are puzzled and disturbed by change. That's why so many of them marry their stenographers; it's in hope of finding the same efficiency at home as at the office. They are supreme optimists.

> If you go into the business world to meet male competition, then you've got to play the game more or less according to their rules. By doing that, I've found that

any intelligent girl can get along very well. About the only important difference I've noticed is in the problem of travel; men can travel alone easier than women. However, old habits of transportation are changing and the comfort of women is more and more the concern of air, railroad and bus travel."

Lombard praised consistency, but 1938 was not a good year for her career. After the problems with *Fools of Scandal*, she decided to turn her attention again to dramas. In 1939, she played opposite of Jimmy Stewart in David O. Selznick's *Made for Each Other*, playing Jane Mason, the new bride of lawyer John Mason. The two encounter trouble when they move in with his mother, who disapproves of the match, and the drama heightens when their infant son contracts pneumonia and almost dies. Lombard followed this performance with *In Name Only*, her only picture with Cary Grant, playing a young widow attracted to an (unknown to her) married man. She learns of his wife following a car accident, and heartache ensues. In 1940's *Vigil in the Night*, Lombard played nurse Anne Lee, who was falsely blamed for her own sister's mistake and forced to give up a lucrative job in a big hospital for a smaller practice in the country.

None of these three films did well, but *They Knew What They Wanted* was the worst of the lot. In it, Lombard once again teamed up with Charles Laughton, who played a wealthy, middle-aged farmer named Tony. He proposed to Amy (played by Lombard) through the mail, and when she arrives at his grape vineyard, she believes that it is his handsome assistant, Joe, who had been writing to her and falls for him. Tony finally wins Amy over, only to lose her again to Joe before finally settling down with her. The movie was too depressing and scandalous (Amy gets pregnant by Joe while married to Tony) for the time, and it was panned by critics and audiences alike.

After this final failure, Lombard returned to comedy, starring in one of the title roles in Alfred Hitchcock's *Mr. and Mrs. Smith*. She and Robert Montgomery play a married couple who suddenly learn that they are not legally wed, and comedy ensues as they try to decide whether to stay together or separate. The film put Lombard firmly back on top of the Hollywood scene.

While Carol Lombard was the consummate actress, she was also the consummate wife and hostess at home. She and Gable never had any children, and whether this was by design, accident, or simply a result of the fact that she died when they'd only been married a few years remains unclear. However, without the distractions that a growing family often produces, she was able to focus on enjoying their private life together during the small amounts of time that their careers allowed them a time of rest and relaxation. Both Lombard and Gable enjoyed the great outdoors, and shortly after their marriage, they bought a 20 acre ranch in Encino, California. It was here that they went for private time away from the prying eyes of tourists taking the classic tour of celebrity homes in Los Angeles or Hollywood. They would also go on hunting trips, and both Gable and Lombard were reported to be good shots capable of bringing home meat for the table. They even kept barnyard animals, perhaps allowing Lombard to recreate some of her earliest, happiest childhood memories from Fort Wayne.

Both Gable and Lombard enjoyed entertaining, regularly having friends out to the ranch for the weekend or longer. With the help of a small staff, Lombard enjoyed giving dinner parties, and she regularly spoke to reporters about the fun of casual, comfortable get-togethers. She even went out of her way to combat the glamorous image that so many other actresses of that era sought to cultivate, saying, "I can't imagine a duller fate than being the best dressed woman in reality. When I want to do something I don't pause to contemplate whether I'm exquisitely gowned. I want to live, not pose!" She would later add, "Personally, I resent being tagged 'glamour girl.' It's such an absurd, extravagant label. It implies so much that I'm not."

Instead, she praised the simplicity and comfort of the then popular hostess gown, a classic, floor length dress often made of similar fabrics in typical evening clothes. Unlike many of the most popular and fashionable garments of the day, it followed a woman's natural lines and figure, allowing her to live comfortably during her own party. Lombard loved them, saying "An at-home costume or hostess gown is absolutely essential for the woman who entertains, and for two reasons. First, this type of costume is extremely flattering, and that does wonders for any woman's poise, and secondly, it eliminates the possibility of appearing overdressed in case a guest shows up in a simple daytime outfit. If a woman has a limited wardrobe, it would be wise to sacrifice a second dinner or evening frock for one hostess gown. She'll soon rate it the most valuable asset in her clothes collection."

Chapter 9: Pay Your Share

"All of which sums up to this. Play fair and be reasonable. When a woman can do that, she'll make some man the best manager he ever found, or wind up running a whole department store. And being a woman, thank heaven you still have that choice! Nobody likes a man who is always fumbling when it's time to pay the check. I think the woman who assumes that the man can afford to pay for everything is making a mistake. More and more the custom of the Dutch treat is coming in vogue, particularly among working men and women. You don't have to surrender your femininity if you pay your share of the bills." – Carole Lombard

Though raised in Los Angeles, Lombard was born in Indiana and would in many ways always be an all-American girl. This was on display in her patriotic statements, especially during the desperate years of the Depression. She once shocked reporters by saying that she wanted to make more pictures so she could make more money and pay more taxes, explaining, "If I can give the government a quarter of 1 million bucks a year, who's better off for it? Certainly I'm no worse off for working--pardon me, did I say working? I mean for doing something like this instead of pouring coffee in a canteen." And though her personal life would never be confused for that of a nun's, she was reverent in her own way and maintained a belief in God, no doubt learned in her early years in Sunday school. Though her faith was of a different nature than most Americans', she once described it: "I don't seem to get solemn about it, and some people might not understand. That's why I never talk about it. I think it's all here– in the mountains and the desert. I don't think God is a softie, either. In the end, it's better if people are forced back into– well– into being right, before they're too far gone. I think your temple is your everyday living."

Given her love for country and her belief in "paying her own way", it is no surprise that Lombard became almost immediately involved in war bond rallies once the United States entered World War II. In early January 1942, just weeks after the Pearl Harbor attacks, Lombard flew with her mother to her home state for a war bond rally. These rallies were springing up across the country as celebrities appeared before adoring fans to entertain them and then encourage them to buy government-issued bonds to help finance the American war effort. Lombard proved to be a natural at this, and she raised a record-breaking $2 million in bond sales in just one evening.

Otto Winkler, Clark Gable's press agent, was traveling with Lombard and Peters on this trip, and he made arrangements for them to return to California by train. However, Lombard was anxious to get back home to Gable and begin filming her latest movie, *They All Kissed the Bride*, so she proposed that the three take a commercial flight instead of the multi-day train trip home. Winkler and her mother both disagreed, as they were both afraid of flying and had already made travel plans.

Undeterred, Lombard persuaded Peters and Winkler to flip a coin to decide what to do, and she won the coin toss, so the three departed the next morning at 4:00 a.m. on January 16 aboard TWA Flight 3. Upon hearing that their idol would be flying out of their local airport, some of Lombard's most devoted fans followed the party right up to the edge of the runway. After gracefully ascending the stairs of the plane, Lombard turned at the door and faced her fans. With a big smile and wave, she called out, "Before I say goodbye to you all, come on and join me in a big cheer! V for Victory!"

Lombard with her mother and Winkler

The plane made good time from Indiana as it headed west, but while refueling in Albuquerque, Lombard and her group were removed from the list of passengers to make room for servicemen. Lombard protested that they should be allowed to stay on because of their work at the war bond rallies, and as a result, the flight crew removed other civilian passengers. The flight then made its way to Las Vegas, where it landed and refueled on the evening of January 16. It then took off again as scheduled at 7:07 p.m. Pacific time, and according to witnesses, the plane rose and flew west for about 20 minutes. Then, tragically, the plane hit an unusually high snowdrift on Potosi Mountain and crashed, killing everyone aboard.

Though the Army acted quickly to secure the site from prying eyes, reporters nonetheless flew in from all parts of the country to get a look at the crash site, and one man described the scene: "The totally demolished luxurious Douglas DC-3 Skyclub presented a grim, sorrowful picture on its rocky resting place. Wreckage was scattered in a radius of 500 yards and some of the victims were strewn around the waist-high snow. Bits of the plane, personal effects of the passengers, including handkerchiefs, overcoats and other apparel, were strung from the branches of stunted pine trees like macabre Christmas ornaments."

Upon hearing about the crash and his wife's death, Gable flew to Las Vegas and was taken to the site, where he joined other searchers looking for the bodies of the lost. As a result, he was there when Lombard's crumpled corpse was found, and the next day, January 18, he returned with Lombard's body, that of her mother, and that of his close friend Winkler, to Los Angeles. The Army, devastated at the loss, wanted to honor Lombard with a full military funeral, but Gable refused and instead followed the wishes that Lombard had already laid out in her will: "I request that no person other than my immediate family and the persons who shall prepare my remains for interment be permitted to view my remains after death has been pronounced. I further request a private funeral and that I be clothed in white and placed in a modestly priced crypt in Forest Lawn Memorial Park, Glendale, California." That's the way it was done, with a simple stone added later, marking the grave of "Carole Lombard Gable."

Within hours of her death, eulogies and accolades poured in for Lombard from all over the country. President Roosevelt told the press, "She brought great joy to all who knew her and to millions who knew her only as a great artist. She gave unselfishly of time and talent to serve her government in peace and war. She loved her country. She is and always will be a star, one we shall never forget, nor cease to be grateful to." Fellow actress Barbara Stanwyck bemoaned her passing, saying, "She was so alive, modern, frank, and natural that she stands out like a beacon on a lightship in this odd place called Hollywood." Meanwhile, David Shipman gushed, "There is a strong case to be made for the divinity of Carole Lombard. One is certain that at Olympian banquets, she's right up there next to Zeus."

For his part, Gable never fully recovered from her early death. The death plunged him into a deep depression, and despite finishing the film in which he was acting at the time, *Somewhere I'll Find You* (1942), Gable was ultimately unable to mask his heartbreak and even lost 20 pounds. Actress Esther Williams pointed out that after Lombard's death, Gable "was never the same. His heart sank a bit." He would later tell friends that in addition to losing his wife that day, he also lost his best friend.

Despite the fact his wife had died in a plane crash, within just a few months, he joined the United States Air Force, training for and then performing numerous combat missions across Europe. In fact, Gable joined the war at his own wife's request shortly before her death, and though he would later marry twice more, everyone who knew him maintained that Carol Lombard was the one true love of his life. He himself confirmed this when he left instructions that, upon his death, he was to be interred next to her in Forest Lawn.

Chapter 10: Be Feminine

"All of this, does not keep you from preserving your femininity. You can still be insane about a particular brand of perfume, and weep when you get a run in your favorite pair of stockings. You can still have fits when the store sends out the very shade of red drapes you did not order, and which swear horribly at the red in the davenport. But when you go down to complain, be a man about it." – Carole Lombard

When Carol Lombard died, her final film, *To Be or Not to Be*, had just been completed and was in post-production. The movie, a satiric look at the Nazis, also starred Jack Benny, and years later, a more famous version of the same film would be made by Mel Brooks. The director, Ernst Lubitsch, decided to complete and release the film with a few small changes. Specifically, one of Lombard's seemingly prophetic lines, "What can happen on a plane?", was cut. In spite of the interest that had been generated by her untimely death, the film did not do well, but critics praised Lombard's performance and agreed that it was a perfect capstone to her stellar, though short, career.

Joan Crawford replaced Lombard in *They All Kissed The Bride*, and in recognition of her predecessor's contribution to the war effort, Crawford donated her entire salary to the American Red Cross. The Red Cross had been involved in the search for the bodies of Lombard and the others following the plane crash that took her life. It then assisted the families of those aboard, especially those of the servicemen killed, via shipping bodies and making funeral arrangements.

In the months immediately following her death, various military and patriotic groups asked permission to erect memorials to Lombard at the site of the crash and in other places around the country. Clark Gable consistently turned down these requests until 1943, when the United States Maritime Commission asked his permission to name their newest Liberty Ship the *Carole Lombard*. Gable not only agreed to the ship's new name but also attended the launch on January 15, 1944, just two short years after Lombard's magnificent bond raising event. The ship served in the Pacific throughout the rest of the war, rescuing hundreds of American sailors who had survived their ships being bombed and/or sank.

Of course, Hollywood offered her no shortages of memorials or commemorations. In 1999, Carol Lombard was named one of the 50 greatest actresses of the 20th century by the American Film Institute, and she has long had a star on the Hollywood Walk of Fame. Her home in Fort Wayne, Indiana, is now a designated historic landmark, and a nearby bridge is called the Carole Lombard Memorial Bridge.

In the 70 years since Lombard's death, actresses and other celebrities have become more and more famous for their bad behavior rather than what they do for the good of others. Carole Lombard was no saint, and she would be the first to laugh at (and probably curse out) anyone who implied that she was. However, she also knew how to act gracefully when the situation called for it. And though she was a star of the screwball comedy, she died on her way home from one of the most important and serious performances of her life: raising money for her country. As the last few days of her life made clear, she was hardly a stereotype.

Marilyn Monroe

Chapter 1: The Mystery of Norma Jean Baker

"Dogs never bite me. Just humans." – Marilyn Monroe

Marilyn Monroe would be an enigma for much of her life, and the mysteries started with her birth certificate. It's well known that she went by the name Norma Jean Baker before Marilyn Monroe, but her name on the birth certificate was Norma Jeane Mortenson. Her mother was Gladys Pearl Baker, whose last name Baker had come from her first marriage. When Norma Jeane was born, Martin E. Mortensen was Gladys's second husband. They had been married in 1924 and would remain legally bound through part of 1927. However, both Gladys and Marilyn Monroe apparently believed Mortensen was not the father, which begs the question of why Gladys had not simply given her newborn daughter her own maiden name for a last name. It's also unclear why the birth certificate misspelled Mortensen's last name.

REGISTRATION 1901	CERTIFIED COPY OF BIRTH RECORD	REGISTRAR'S NUMBER 7791
NAME OF CHILD—FIRST NAME NORMA	MIDDLE NAME JEANE	LAST NAME MORTENSON
SEX FEMALE	DATE OF BIRTH—MONTH, DAY, YEAR Jun. 1, 1926	
PLACE OF BIRTH—CITY OR TOWN LOS ANGELES		PLACE OF BIRTH—COUNTY LOS ANGELES
MAIDEN NAME OF MOTHER GLADYS MONROE		COLOR OR RACE WHITE
NAME OF FATHER EDWARD MORTENSON		COLOR OR RACE WHITE
DATE RECEIVED BY LOCAL REGISTRAR Jun. 5, 1926		DATE(S) OF CORRECTION(S), IF ANY

This is to certify, that the foregoing is a true and correct copy of statements appearing on the record of birth of the above named child, as filed in this office

SIGNATURE AND CERTIFICATE OF George M. Weil, M.D.	HEALTH Officer & Registrar
PLACE OF CERTIFICATION LOS ANGELES, CALIFORNIA	DATE CERTIFIED Oct. 24, 1955
STATE OF CALIFORNIA	REV 7-1-49 FORM H-83-61	DEPARTMENT OF PUBLIC HEALTH

Marilyn Monroe's birth certificate

While there is no conclusive answer, it is likely that Norma Jean was born out of wedlock, and that Gladys had been involved in too many affairs for her to know who the father was with any certainty. Marilyn would later recall her mother showing her a picture of a man named Charles Stanley Gifford, and coming to believe Gifford was her father. Since Gifford partially resembled Clark Gable, it was good enough for the young girl.

In the 1920s, it would have been highly unusual if not socially unacceptable to give her daughter her maiden name. Given this dilemma, Gladys apparently chose the more socially respectable solution of using the name of her previous husband, even though they had been separated well before she was pregnant with Norma Jean. And Norma Jeane Mortensen became Norma Jean Baker due to the fact that she had also separated from Mortensen prior to her daughter's birth. On her daughter's birth certificate, Gladys listed Martin E. Mortensen's residence as "unknown".

Gladys Pearl Baker lived an unfortunate life, plagued with an unstable neurological profile that would unfortunately leave an imprint on her daughter's life. Norma Jean was her third child, following two children with first husband Jack Baker. The eldest child, Hermitt Jack, died of tuberculosis while still an infant. the second child, Bernice Baker, was born in 1919 and raised by Jack Baker, who removed his daughter from Gladys's possession when the two ended their marriage.

Gladys Baker

Gladys's turbulent relationships with men were indicative of her wildly unpredictable disposition, which made it impossible to depend on her to perform even the elementary tasks associated with raising a child. Her own upbringing was every bit as tumultuous as Norma Jean's would be; Gladys's mother showed no interest in her, and her father suffered from dementia. Gladys had a long history of mental illness in her family, and one of her grandfathers committed suicide. As she grew older, Gladys grew more and more mentally disabled, which was partly a result of a self-fulfilling prophecy, because she had spent her early years living in fear of acquiring the kind of mental illnesses that ran in the family.

The decision to give Norma Jean the last name of her second husband is understandable. Even though they had already separated, the two were still technically married until 1928. However, there is little reason to believe that Mortensen was actually the biological father of Norma Jean. After just four months into their marriage, Gladys had separated from Mortensen under the pretense that he was too dull. Always erratic, she had difficulty attaching herself to one man, and she quickly moved on to a string of affairs that made it all but impossible to identify Norma Jean's father. Like Marilyn herself believed, recent scholars think Gifford was her father. Gifford and Gladys had worked together during her brief stint as a film cutter.

While the identity of her father will never be definitively verified, it is certain that Norma Jean was born at Los Angeles County Hospital on June 1, 1926. Shortly after her birth, Gladys changed her daughter's last name to "Baker," despite the fact that Marilyn would never develop any relationship with Jack Baker. More difficult for Gladys than deciding on a name was figuring out who should raise her daughter. Gladys wanted to raise her child, but she could not give up her job. As Donald Spoto states in his biography of Marilyn, there was also a stigma against single mothers at the time, and Gladys was influenced by a Puritanical ethos that discriminated against children who were born out of wedlock:

> "Other factors encouraged Gladys to place the baby with a 'decent' family: she could not quit her job, there was no one to care for Norma Jean while she worked, and her restless, nomadic life (like her mother's as she may have apprehended) was unsuitable for mothering."

It's somewhat surprising that Gladys, who had always possessed a reckless character, would be influenced by social customs to the extent that she would relinquish control of her daughter. But that was probably part and parcel of Gladys's instability; she could be socially proper one minute and entirely irascible the next.

On June 13, just 12 days after her birth, Norma Jean moved in with Ida and Albert Bolender. The contrast between the Bolenders and Gladys was incredibly stark. While Gladys was viewed as a figure of ill repute, the Bolenders upheld traditional moral values, providing the kind of stable environment Gladys could never have offered. Albert worked as a postman, while Ida tended the house. Like many families during the 1920s and the Great Depression, the Bolenders also made money by raising foster children, a task for which they were given $25 per month for each child. Although it is unclear how many foster children lived with the Bolenders at a time, the living quarters were definitely tight in their small four-room bungalow in Los Angeles. For her part, Gladys was resolute in her commitment to her daughter, and she always paid the $25 monthly expense afforded to the Bolenders.

For the most part, Norma Jean's early years were comfortable, but living in close proximity to Gladys and Norma Jean's grandmother Della occasionally posed difficulties. In one episode in 1927, Della visited the Bolenders' house and demanded to see Norma Jean. Ida refused, leading Della to break the door open with her elbow, after which she walked to Norma Jean's crib and nearly strangled Norma Jean with a pillow. In a similar incident years later, Gladys visited the Bolenders in an attempt to take her daughter. After Albert and Ida refused, Gladys stuffed her young daughter in a large duffel bag and only relinquished Norma Jean after the Bolenders wrestled the duffel bag from Gladys's possession.

Naturally, these events ensured that there was substantial animosity between Norma Jean's biological family and her foster parents. However, while she received little personal attention from the Bolenders, she was well provided for at a time in which many children nationwide were without basic needs. She was also a well-adjusted child, attending the Ballona Elementary and Kindergarten and subsequently the Vine Street Elementary School in Hawthorne, Los Angeles.

By 1933, Gladys's health had improved, and she was economically sufficient enough to qualify for a housing loan. She purchased a house in Hollywood and continued to care for Della, which she had done for the past several years. But as 1933 progressed, Della became ill with acute heart pulmonary disorder. Wanting her daughter to live with Della during her final years, Gladys took back Norma Jean, who had been classified as a ward of the state. The young girl didn't mind, because she still had a good relationship with Gladys and she thought life with the Bolenders was dull. In fact, she would later recount a dream that sheds light on the repression she felt while living with the Bolenders: "I dreamed that I was standing up in church, without any clothes on, and all the people there were lying at my feet on the floor of the church, and I walked naked, with a sense of freedom, over their prostrate forms, being careful not to step on anyone".

It is apparent that Norma Jean was not terribly interested in religion, and continuing to live with her foster parents would have likely led to unhappiness. She had also been saddened by the death of her dog, Tippy, who had been shot by a neighbor earlier in 1933. Moving in with Gladys and Della appeared to offer a refreshing change of scenery.

Chapter 2: School Years

"I think Marilyn is bound to make an almost overwhelming impression on the people who meet her for the first time. It is not that she is pretty, although she is of course almost incredibly pretty, but she radiates, at the same time, unbounded vitality and a kind of unbelievable innocence. I have met the same in a lion-cub, which my native servants in Africa brought me. I would not keep her, since I felt that it would in some way be wrong...I shall never forget the almost overpowering feeling of unconquerable strength and sweetness which she conveyed. I had all the wild nature of Africa amicably gazing at me with mighty playfulness." – Author Isak Dinesen, 1961

While living with Gladys, Marilyn continued to attend Vine Street Elementary School. However, Gladys's mother died, and her father then hung himself. Losing her parents in rapid succession had a crippling effect on her, and Gladys was hospitalized just a few months after taking Norma Jean back. Marilyn would later note that her mother was "screaming and laughing" as she was taken away to the hospital. Gladys would never again be able to live independently, and she spent the majority of the rest of her life hospitalized. Her finances were possessed in 1935, and her daughter was permanently displaced from her supervision.

One of the more peculiar aspects of Norma Jean's upbringing is that even though she was separated from her mother, she was never far from her orbit. After Gladys was hospitalized in early 1934, Norma Jean lived with Gladys's best friend, Grace McKee. She would continue to attend the same school, and she received substantially more personal attention from Grace than she had with the Bolenders. Another benefit from Norma Jean's perspective was that Grace refrained from inflicting religion on her.

This period would be one of the happiest of Norma Jean's life, and also relevant to her later career because it fostered her interest in movies. Grace was an avid moviegoer and took young Norma Jean with her on a regular basis. Cinema was a popular form of entertainment throughout the Great Depression; along with sports, films were one of the few affordable forms of entertainment available to everyone. Movies were especially popular among people living near Hollywood, naturally. Baseball had not yet shifted west, and the film industry was already well settled in Los Angeles. Grace and Norma Jean were fans of the movies, and they happened to be living at cinema's epicenter.

The early 1930s were also an opportune time to live in Hollywood, because the movie industry thrived during the decade. Classic genres, including the gangster film, Western, slapstick comedy, and musical, all gained popularity during the decade. Directors like Frank Capra, John Ford, Charlie Chaplin, and Ernst Lubitsch produced hit films, while movie stars achieved even greater fame. Grace and Norma Jean were particularly fond of Jean Harlow, the star of *The Platinum Blond* (1931) and *Public Enemy* (1931). In fact, it was around 1935 that Norma Jean dropped the "e" from her last name, apparently in homage to her favorite actress. Jean Harlow was an ironic if fitting role model for young Norma Jean; Harlow was one of the original "blond bombshells" in Hollywood, and she also died a sudden and premature death at the age of 26.

Enraptured by her favorite films, Grace made her surrogate daughter as glamorous as possible, dressing Norma Jean up in elaborate costumes that mimicked the outfits worn on screen. Grace encouraged Norma Jean to behave in a feminine manner and to take pride in her appearance. As

Spoto notes:

> "But with Grace as tutor…The girl was routinely taken to a beauty parlor, Grace standing by anxiously as curlers, irons and brushes attempted the proleptic glamorization of Norma Jean. She was sometimes hauled into the ladies' lavatory at a tearoom or movie theater and shown the proper application techniques of face powder and lip rouge; eyeliner and a delicate cologne completed a spectacle passersyby could only have regarded as the slightly bizarre, premature display of a pre-adolescent."

Although Grace and Norma Jean were perhaps a bit extreme in their enthusiasm, that kind of behavior was emblematic of America's fascination with cinema during the 1930s. Even though poverty was prominently on display across the country, the screen was filled with extreme images of glamour, and people wanted to indulge themselves in as much of it as they could afford.

In 1935, Grace became the legal guardian of both Norma Jean and Gladys. That same year, Grace married a man named Doc Goddard, which resulted in Norma Jean leaving for the Los Angeles Orphans Home, nicknamed Hollygrove. There were many families that would have been happy to adopt her, but Gladys's persistent refusal left Norma Jean living at the orphanage for two years. While there, Grace continued to take her to the movies and visited her on weekends. After having attended Selma Street Elementary School during 1934 and 1935, she went back to Vine Street Elementary from 1935-1937. In later years, Marilyn would call her time in the orphanage traumatic, but every indication suggests that the period was actually one of stability, particularly compared to the time she spent living with Gladys.

After roughly two years in the Los Angeles Orphans Home, Norma Jean moved in with Doc and Grace during the spring of 1937. While living with her adopted parents, she switched schools, attending Lankershim Elementary School. For the most part, she enjoyed her time with Doc and Grace, but it is now widely believed that she was sexually assaulted by Doc during this time. Oddly enough, when she was not being abused by Doc, Norma Jean was fairly well taken care of, and she continued to progress through school.

Eventually, Grace and Doc were unable to continue caring for Norma Jean, so the teenager moved in with Grace's aunt Olive. This arrangement quickly proved untenable because she was sexually assaulted by Olive's son. Finally, in November 1938, it was decided that she would live with Grace's aunt, Ana Lower.

Ana Lower was 58 years old, and though her health was not strong, she held strict Christian values and raised Norma Jean with a firm hand. With her "Aunt Ana," Norma Jean attended Christian Science meetings, but there is no indication that this was met with hostility. At this point, Norma Jean was still extremely shy, and her body had not yet developed. But during the fall of 1939, when she was 13, her body underwent a swift change and grew to her adult height of 5 foot 5 ½ inches. Prior to her growth spurt, Norma Jean had been rail-thin and lacked confidence. Still a brunette, Norma Jean would still bear little resemblance to her adult self even after getting taller, but she was quickly acquiring the body that would make her famous.

Norma Jean continued to stay with Ana Lower through much of 1942, but by then it became obvious that Ana's health made it impossible for her to continue taking care of Norma Jean during her remaining high school years. Making matters even more complicated, Grace and Doc Goddard decided to move to West Virginia, where Doc had been offered employment, so they could not afford to have Norma Jean move in with them. Norma Jean was just 16 years of age and had not yet reached legal age, but Grace realized that if she married a man who was already 18, she could live with him and avoid moving in with her mother. Since December 1941, Norma Jean had been involved in a relationship with a classmate two years her senior, James Dougherty. Well aware of their relationship, Grace approached James's mother, and the two planned for James to marry Norma Jean. James and Norma Jean were engaged in May of 1942 and married the following month.

The decision for Norma Jean to marry at the age of 16 was complex, and even in retrospect it is difficult to arrive at an optimal solution for her predicament. On the surface, it would seem preferable for Norma Jean to have moved to West Virginia with Grace, the only stable mother figure she'd ever had. However, Norma Jean had apparently already been sexually assaulted by Doc, so moving in with Grace and Doc would have been difficult. While she could have been placed in the custody of her mother, Gladys's mood swings often made her malicious, and living with her was virtually impossible. Marrying her classmate ensured economic security because she was financially supported by James and his mother, and it is not difficult to understand the rationale informing the decision for marriage.

The overriding issue with the marriage was that despite having dated James for over six months, Norma Jean was still shy and socially underdeveloped. In fact, her shyness was part of one of the great paradoxes of the Marilyn Monroe legend and legacy: the contrast between her illustrious physical attributes and her unassuming social conduct. At first glance, it's easy to question how someone as physically beautiful as Norma Jean could lack confidence, but she later claimed, "No one ever told me I was pretty when I was a little girl." Norma Jean had looks that made most of her contemporaries jealous, but she did not have the social graces to appear comfortable in her own skin. At the age of 16, the brunette Norma Jean Baker was a far cry away from the bubbly and ditzy blond stereotypes that some still associate with Marilyn Monroe today.

As James Dougherty's girlfriend, Norma Jean's time with him was leisurely and cheerful. However, as his wife, she was placed in unfamiliar territory. She continued to be socially insecure, especially around his friends, and she also had no familiarity with household tasks like cooking. 16 year old Norma Jean was effectively robbed of two crucial years that were needed in order for her personality to grow up and match her fully developed body. Robbed of her final two years of high school, Norma Jean was forced into abdicating her own intellectual development in the interests of serving a husband to whom she had not lived with long enough to develop a lasting attraction.

Despite the inherent awkwardness of the situation, however, James was committed to providing for Norma Jean to the best of his ability. Though her lack of household skills irritated him, he treated her with respect, but he dominated the relationship so much that Norma Jean actually referred to him as "Daddy". Norma Jean was also sexually inexperienced and still in the process of recuperating from the repeated episodes of sexual abuse she had suffered during her upbringing. Although she and Dougherty were romantic, their romantic endeavors were never initiated by her, reflecting a dynamic in which she did not possess agency over her body.

The decision for Norma Jean to marry Jim Dougherty was made at a time when the United States was in the midst of World War II. Grace had figured that James would go off to war while Norma Jean would enjoy the shelter of James's mother. However, after James enlisted in the Merchant Marines in 1943, he was stationed in Avalon, an island off the coast of California, and Norma Jean left to live with him instead of staying in Los Angeles. Only after James was shipped to the Pacific did Norma Jean move in with James's mother. This dynamic was difficult because Norma Jean was placed in a situation that approximated her living situation with Ana Lower, despite the fact that she had been living as an "adult" housewife for over a year. As a result, Norma Jean's life from 1942-1943 straddled the line between adolescence and adulthood, stunting her intellectual growth and compromising her self-confidence.

After James left for the Pacific, Norma Jean did her part in assisting the war effort by working at the Radioplane Munitions Factory. This was her first job, and she was paid the minimum wage of $20 per week, a paltry sum considering that each week entailed 60 hours of work. Her primary task involved spraying airplane parts with fire retardant, but she also inspected parachutes. Although the work was banal, her workplace received a stir in the fall of 1944 when photographers from the First Motion Picture Unit arrived at the Radioplane factory to photograph and make movies of the female workers. Captain Ronald Reagan wanted his head photographer, David Conover, to convey the female contribution to the war effort, and during one visit to the factory Conover photographed Norma Jean. Conover was taking pictures for the publication *Yank, the Army Weekly*, and Mrs. James Dougherty didn't make it into an issue, but the picture was retrieved after Marilyn Monroe became famous.

Photograph of Norma Jean from *Yank, The Army Weekly*

The image is striking because it's so different from the countless pictures of Marilyn Monroe that everyone has become accustomed to. Norma Jean's hair has not yet become blond, and her hair is also curly. Furthermore, the picture is decidedly plain; outside of the lipstick, her appearance is very much that of a working girl, far different than the highly composed images that would characterize her roles in films such as *Gentlemen Prefer Blondes* (1953) and *Some Like it Hot* (1959).

Chapter 3: Life in the Public Sphere

"I knew I belonged to the public and to the world, not because I was talented or even beautiful, but because I had never belonged to anything or anyone else." – Marilyn Monroe

In February 1945, Norma Jean decided to leave Radioplane in an effort to make a career out of acting and modeling. In August of that year, she applied for the Blue Book Modeling Agency at the advice of David Conover, who had taken her picture. Once she was accepted, Norma Jean naturally went about mimicking the fashion styles of Lana Turner and her beloved Jean Harlow (who had since died). Norma Jean bleached her hair blond like her two favorite actresses.

Lana Turner and Clark Gable in *Honky Tonk* (1941)

Norma Jean's major breakthrough came when she was featured on the April 1946 cover of *Family Circle* magazine in an image that was shot by renowned photographer Andre de Dienes.

The image conveys an almost awkward innocence, with Norma Jean posing as a milkmaid and clutching a sheep high above her waist. The youthful, almost childlike depiction is surprising in light of the fact that Norma Jean was dating de Dienes at the time the photograph was shot. On the other hand, Norma Jean is portrayed in an affectionate manner that suggests the enthusiasm the photographer felt toward his subject.

Throughout 1946, Norma Jean would appear in a number of magazines, but she still aspired to be a movie star, an ambition instilled in her by Grace several years earlier. In July 1946, she was offered the opportunity to audition for 20th Century Fox, and later that month she was hired by studio executive Ben Lyon and signed to a contract of $75 per week, with the stipulation that after six months the contract could be renewed at a salary of $125 per week. Because she was still under the legal age, Grace was called upon to give her approval, a fitting gesture given that she had been the one who sparked Norma Jean's love for show business.

Ben Lyon

After hiring her, Lyon impressed upon Norma Jean the importance of changing her name. "Norma Jean" was too matronly and had no sex appeal. Lyon liked using the last name Monroe, which was natural for Norma Jean because it was Gladys's maiden name, but picking a first name proved more difficult. In homage to Jean Harlow, "Jean Monroe" was considered as an option until Lyon came up with Marilyn, inspired by the actress Marilyn Miller and a personal superstition that alliterative names brought good fortune. Norma Jean didn't care for the name Marilyn, because it sounded too much like Mary Lynn to her, but from August 1946 onward, Norma Jean Baker was Marilyn Monroe.

The rest of 1946 brought Marilyn continued success and photo features in multiple magazines, but the photo shoots were still a means to an end for Marilyn, who still harbored her childhood dreams of becoming a movie star. However, they are worth analyzing in their own right, if only for the similarities and differences between them and the way she was filmed as an actress. On the surface, Marilyn's brown hair makes her appear almost unrecognizable when compared with her later depictions for the film camera. Ironically, as Richard Dyer points out, Marilyn was conveyed with a simple style that was the antithesis of glamour:

> "The early pin-ups of Monroe belong not to the highly wrought glamour
> traditions of Hollywood, associated with photographers such Ruth Harriet
> Louise and George Hurrell; they below rather to a much simpler and probably
> more common tradition, both in style and choice of model. The style is generally
> head-on, using high-key lighting, few props and vague backdrops; the model is

always young, generally white, the 'healthy, American, cheerleader type'…and not individualized".

One of Marilyn Monroe's early pin-up pictures

While it is true that the early pin-ups offered little glamour, Marilyn's lack of self-consciousness and comfort toward the camera would characterize her movie roles. Still, in light of her controversial persona and film career, it is ironic that Marilyn was portrayed as such an all-American figure.

That same year, Marilyn's personal life underwent a drastic change, as she and James Dougherty divorced in early autumn following his return from the war. The divorce was no surprise, given that she and James had been separated for three years, far longer than the period in which they had even lived together. Marilyn later noted, "My marriage didn't make me sad, but it didn't make me happy either. My husband and I hardly spoke to each other. This wasn't because we were angry. We had nothing to say. I was dying of boredom."

While the divorce was to be expected, it is also fitting that it corresponded with the onset of Marilyn's career, since it seemingly reflected her prioritizing of her career above relationships and the domestic life. In the end, World War II may have liberated Marilyn from a domestic life of obscurity. Marilyn would later famously comment, "I have too many fantasies to be a housewife. I guess I am a fantasy."

In the span of a year, a young brunette housewife named Norma Jean Baker had been transformed into a blond pin-up model with a studio-chosen name. Although these changes sound sweeping, they were not exactly unprecedented in Hollywood during the 1940s. During that decade, Hollywood kept to a fairly narrow framework for their actors and actresses, and in order to achieve success it was necessary for Marilyn to conform to the prevailing template. In 1946, one prime example was Rita Hayworth, who was deployed as a pin-up model for trips overseas and was arguably the most powerful actress in Hollywood at the time Marilyn was signed by 20th Century Fox. Born of Mexican ethnicity, Rita Hayworth's original name was Margarita Cansino, but after signing with Columbia Pictures it was determined that her profile was too ethnic and exotic. As a result, her hair was dyed from brown to dark red, and her name changed to Rita Hayworth. Ironically, Rita Hayworth's transformation was the inverse of Marilyn's; while Hayworth's exoticism was tamed, Marilyn's plainspoken and matronly identity was sexed up. But both examples reflect the way in which achieving film stardom entailed a complex, manufactured process that molded the actress to suit the studio's needs.

Rita Hayworth in 1945

Chapter 4: Starting a Film Career

"Hollywood is a place where they'll pay you a thousand dollars for a kiss and fifty cents for your soul." – Marilyn Monroe

Early in 1947, 20th Century Fox renewed Marilyn's contract for another six months, paying her at a rate of $125 per week. Shortly thereafter, she would appear in her first two films, *The Shocking Miss Pilgrim* (1947) and *Scudda Hoo! Scudda Hay!* (1948). Neither was remarkable, nor were they meant to be since they were small budget films.

The Shocking Miss Pilgrim was a period film set in 1870s London, while *Scudda Hoo! Scudda Hay!* was more significant because it featured Marilyn's first speaking role; she says "Hi, Rad" to the main character, Rad McGill (played by June Haver).

The most prominent film Marilyn would star in for 20th Century Fox was *Dangerous Years* (1948), a film involving teenage mischief. While she did not have a major role, Marilyn had a credited part playing the role of Eve, an employee at a small dance hall. While these initial appearances were modest to say the least, Marilyn obtained more substantial roles as time passed, and her career seemed to be headed in the right direction.

In July 1947, Marilyn had exhausted her time with the studio, and her contract was not renewed, but in March 1948, Marilyn rebounded and signed with Columbia Pictures for a contract that would pay her the same $125 per week rate that she had received from Fox. Shortly after signing with her new studio, Marilyn won the co-starring part in the low-budget film *Ladies of the Chorus* (1949). Directed by Phil Karlsen, the film follows Marilyn as she attempts to avoid repeating the mistakes of her mother, a fitting narrative with obvious parallels to her own life. Unfortunately, the film was so widely panned that Columbia actually dropped Marilyn.

Though she spent a limited amount of time with Columbia, her experience there had two lasting and important consequences. The first was that studio head Harry Cohn altered her overbite. The second and more influential development occurred in April, around the same time that shooting began for *Ladies of the Chorus*. That month, Marilyn met Natasha Lytess, the head drama instructor for Columbia Pictures. The two formed a quick bond, and Lytess would remain with Marilyn for much of her career, long after her departure from Columbia.

The remainder of 1948 was spent in frustration until December, when Marilyn met Johnny Hyde, who became her new agent. Hyde took an immediate interest in Marilyn, but at first he had difficulty finding her film roles. In order to supplement her income, Marilyn was relegated to posing nude for calendar photographs. When later asked if she had actually posed nude, Marilyn would coyly reply, "It's not true I had nothing on. I had the radio on." When asked the question decades later, she would strike a more serious tone, explaining, "The body is meant to be seen, not all covered up."

Even with that additional income, Marilyn couldn't provide for herself. Hyde subsidized Marilyn and effectively mortgaged his own career by gambling on hers. The Monroe-Hyde partnership failed to produce any immediate success, but Marilyn was able to secure roles in several low-budget films.

Early in 1949, Johnny Hyde paid for Marilyn to have plastic surgery on her nose. While it is impossible to determine the extent to which the plastic surgery altered the course of her career, Marilyn received her most significant role months later in October, when she was cast for the part of Angela Phinlay in John Huston's *The Asphalt Jungle* (1950). Huston was a major Hollywood director at the time, having made classics like *The Maltese Falcon* (1941) and *Key Largo* (1942). His punchy style involved dramatic, tension-filled scenes, and his films attracted a wide audience. Receiving a credit in a John Huston film was a major achievement, and it immediately elevated her standing in Hollywood. In her role, Marilyn portrayed the niece of a corrupt lawyer involved in a jewel heist. Playing the part of a gangster's moll was far different than the succession of light-hearted characters she would later portray. Her physical attributes and tight black dress certainly fulfilled the requisite seductiveness needed for her role, but she may very well have not been cast in such a role after her star persona had already been established.

Marilyn in *Asphalt Jungle*

Both *Asphalt Jungle* and Marilyn's role in the film garnered rave reviews, and she would not have to wait long before landing her next significant role. In early spring of 1950, Johnny Hyde introduced her to Joseph Mankiewicz, who was still a relatively unknown director of B-movies but was about to become one of the most famous directors in Hollywood. Mankiewicz was in the process of casting for *All About Eve*, a film that would be his largest to date. After meeting Marilyn, Mankiewicz agreed to cast her in the part of Claudia Caswell, a role representing an almost hyperbolic rendering of the dumb blonde stereotype. Although the role was Marilyn's largest up to that point, her character set the tone for the types of roles she would later play.

Even if *All About Eve* did not portray Marilyn in an intellectually favorable light, the film is still worth seeing, if only for its significance in Marilyn's early career. It stars Bette Davis as Margo Channing, an aging actress who is emulated by a younger actress named Eve (played by Anne Baxter). As Claudia Caswell, Marilyn's character lacks the grace of Eve and the drama of Margo, existing as a purely one-dimensional character whose only purpose is to be admired for her looks and mocked for her absolute lack of intellect.

One famous scene in the film illustrates the brainlessness of Claudia. While at a party, Claudia is introduced by theater critic Addison DeWitt (George Sanders) as an aspiring starlet who had graduated from the "Copacabana School of Dramatic Art." The viewer is encouraged to laugh at Claudia, since it is self-evident that no such school exists. Later in the scene, Marilyn's character is again mocked. In a long-take featuring her, George Sanders, Bette Davis, and Anne Baxter, Marilyn stands in the background while the other characters converse. The effect is as though Marilyn were a background ornament to admire while the "important" characters talk amongst themselves in the foreground. When she finally speaks, her lines are bits of stereotypical dumb-blonde dialogue. Her character exists to be laughed at, and to call attention to the superior intellect of the other characters.

A still photo from *All About Eve*

All About Eve did not portray Marilyn's character in a positive light, but her career still owed a great deal to the film. She received far more screen time than any other film she had appeared in, and she delivered a substantial amount of dialogue as well, easily dwarfing the number of lines she had given in *Asphalt Jungle*. If anything, Marilyn might not have been typecast in her later roles as a dumb blond had it not been for *All About Eve*. After all, in *Dangerous Years* and *Asphalt Jungle*, Marilyn had portrayed characters who were not only smarter but also more threatening. While *All About Eve* was instrumental in the development of Marilyn Monroe as a star actress, the fame it brought her also ended up pigeonholing her into a relatively narrow typecast for future film roles. Some subsequent films would incorporate Marilyn Monroe because she was a star, not because the kind of role she played was vital to success.

The success of *All About Eve* launched Marilyn's career to new heights, and in December 1950 she signed a contract with 20th Century Fox, the same studio that had released her three years earlier. However, the end of the year also brought unfortunate news. Johnny Hyde, the agent responsible for her roles in *Asphalt Jungle* and *All About Eve*, died just 8 days after her new contract with 20th Century Fox was signed. Johnny's death was a big loss for Marilyn, as he had treated her better than any other man in her life up to that point. Without Johnny, Marilyn had difficulty securing roles during the beginning of 1951, although she was called upon to present at the Academy Awards that year. She also took courses at UCLA, studying literature and art appreciation.

Marilyn's big break in 1951 was not actually a film appearance but instead a party that she attended. At the party, she met studio president Spyros Skouras, who was captivated by her appearance. Following that party, Marilyn was signed to a 7 year contract with Fox. In an example of life imitating art, it is difficult not to see the parallels between Marilyn's attendance at the Fox studio party and her role in *All About Eve*. In both cases, she is noted almost entirely based on her physical appearance, a dynamic she had trouble distancing herself from during her career.

Spyros Skouras

Over the remainder of 1951, Marilyn would appear in several insignificant films. Her first movie during her new contract with Fox was *Let's Make it Legal*, a romantic comedy addressing domesticity and whether a man and woman should get a divorce. It was not until 1952 that Marilyn appeared in more substantial roles, but the fall of 1951 was still significant because Marilyn was featured in a story in *Collier's* magazine titled "Hollywood's 1951 Model Blonde." The story detailed her rise to fame, with special attention paid to her meeting with Spyrous Skouras. Another notable aspect of the story was the magazine cover; though Marilyn had previously been photographed only in pin-up photographs, the magazine's cover portrayed her in a party dress (no doubt a reference to the studio party), a less overtly sexual pose that implied that there was more to Marilyn than just her looks.

Although she had not yet reached the heights of her stardom, 1952 was the busiest year of Marilyn's career. She appeared in five films: *O. Henry's Full House*, *Monkey Business*, *Clash By Night*, *We're Not Married!*, and *Don't Bother to Knock*. The stature of the films also increased.

She only had one starring role, but Marilyn acted in films directed by luminaries like Howard Hawks and Fritz Lang. For Hawks, she appeared in *O. Henry's Full House* (a film adaptation of five O. Henry stories) and *Monkey Business*, the latter of which was one of the most acclaimed films of the year and one of Hawks' most popular films. In *Monkey Business*, Marilyn plays the secretary for Cary Grant, whose character is in the midst of a mid-life crisis. Although filled with moments of slapstick comedy, the film takes an uncompromising look at marriage and the difficulties of growing old. Marilyn was cast in a role every bit as demeaning as her appearance in *All About Eve*, but that was more expected in a comedy. Even still, it probably cemented the archetype that Marilyn found herself.

Marilyn did manage to appear in two dramatic roles in 1952, portraying significant characters in *Clash By Night* and *Don't Bother to Knock*. Directed by Fritz Lang, *Clash By Night* explores the claustrophobia that can result from living in a small town. Although Marilyn was not the main star, her portrayal as Peggy, the frustrated girlfriend of a domineering boyfriend, earned positive reviews, as did the film. An early scene illustrates the stark difference between her role and the stereotypical characters she portrayed in *All About Eve* and *Monkey Business*. Unlike her earlier films, Marilyn appears in a working-girls outfit of jeans and a button-down blouse, a stark departure from the dress she had worn in *All About Eve*. After her boyfriend criticizes her for eating a candy bar and tells her, "You'll spread", Peggy engages in a mock fight with him, indicating her refusal to submit to the conventions of patriarchy.

Marilyn as Peggy in *Clash By Night*

Although it is largely forgotten today, *Don't Bother to Knock* gave Marilyn her first starring role. Marilyn plays a mentally unstable babysitter who had previously attempted to kill herself. After she accepts a man's solicitation from across the hall, she draws the ire of the father of the children she is supposed to watch. Although her character is psychologically unstable, she is strong-willed and refuses to submit to either the man from across the hall or the father of the children. *Don't Bother to Knock* has eerie parallels with Marilyn's personal life, including her own psychological unrest and suicidal tendencies.

Chapter 5: Making It Big

"When you're famous you kind of run into human nature in a raw kind of way. It stirs up envy, fame does. People you run into feel that, well, who does she think she is, Marilyn Monroe? They feel fame gives them some kind of privilege to walk up to you and say anything to you, of any kind of nature — and it won't hurt your feelings — like it's happening to your clothes not you." – Marilyn Monroe

By the end of 1952, Marilyn had become one of the premier stars in Hollywood, and her film roles in 1953 were even more substantial. Marilyn played major parts in *Gentlemen Prefer Blondes*, *Niagara*, and *How to Marry a Millionaire*. Most notable among these was *Gentlemen Prefer Blondes*, a film that is often considered to be the finest in which she appeared. Renewing her professional relationship with Howard Hawks, Marilyn was cast in the role of Anita Loo and co-starred with Jane Russell, who portrayed Dorothy Shaw. Anita and Dorothy are best friends who have opposite personalities; while Anita is a gold-digger, Dorothy looks for a man who is virtuous and will offer her security. The film relied on Marilyn's singing and dancing training and features several musical numbers, including the legendary "Diamonds are a Girl's Best Friend." Although Anita wishes to marry a rich gentleman, his mother will not allow him to marry her because she believes Anita is not smart enough. Finally, at the film's conclusion, Anita convinces her beau that she is intellectually adept enough to be his wife.

Marilyn Monroe performing "Diamonds Are a Girl's Best Friend"

Gentlemen Prefer Blondes is perhaps the most challenging film in which Marilyn appeared, with many contradictions that make its message vastly different from what one would expect at first glance. The narrative parallels the trajectory of Marilyn's own life and career, particularly because it involves an attempt to overcome the dumb blonde label to which she has been assigned. At first glance, Anita would appear to represent the worst manifestation of the stereotypical "Marilyn" character, as she communicates slowly and with a high-pitched voice that make it seem as though she has no ability to communicate. Additionally, *Gentlemen Prefer Blondes* appears to privilege patriarchy, as the narrative is superficially predicated on Marilyn's attempt to prove that she is worthy of her prospective husband. However, a close reading of the film reveals that it is far more balanced in its gender portrayal. In particular, the relationship between Marilyn and Jane Russell is the dominant grouping, and Marilyn's gold-digging is more likely an attempt to subsidize her relationship with her best friend. In this regard, the film subverts dominant gender conventions even though it appears to subscribe to them.

In many ways, *How to Marry a Millionaire* borrowed from *Gentlemen Prefer Blondes*, with a plot centering on a trio of women who attempt to marry rich men. However, the film does not offer the subversion of *Gentlemen*, since it fails to convey Marilyn with any identity distinct from the male she is to marry. The other film Marilyn made in 1953, *Niagara*, was as an outlier in her career. Marilyn portrays a femme fatale who plans to murder her husband while vacationing at Niagara Falls. In some respects, the film is similar to *Asphalt Jungle*, but the comedic aspects of the earlier film are absent. The film is not well-known today, likely a result of both the movie itself and the somewhat bizarre cinematography choices. The film is one of the only ones in the noir genre shot in Technicolor.

Marilyn Monroe in *Niagra*

By 1954, Marilyn had solidified her place among Hollywood's powerful actors and actresses. However, the highly sexualized characters portrayed in films such as *Gentlemen Prefer Blondes* and *Niagara* were controversial in conservative 1950s America. Marilyn's characters would have been more readily tolerated in the 1920s, but her persona was seen by many Americans as distasteful. At the same time, Marilyn offered an antidote to a society that repressed sexuality. To this end, Richard Dyer contends that Marilyn pushed sexuality into the public sphere, where it had previously remained hidden:

> "in the fifties, there were specific ideas about what sexuality meant and it was held to matter a great deal; and because Marilyn Monroe acted out those specific ideas, and because they were *felt* to matter so much, she was charismatic, a centre of attraction who seemed to embody what was taken to be a central feature of human existence at the time".

Existing as a public figure, Marilyn facilitated the emergence of discourses on sexuality, and indeed Dyer notes that her films can be viewed in tandem with major developments such as the creation of *Playboy* magazine and the publication of the Kinsey reports on male and female sexuality that were published in 1948 and 1953.

Unlike 1953, 1954 is best remembered not for the films in which she appeared but for developments in her personal life. Marilyn appeared in two films, *River of No Return* (a Western that drew from the plot elements of *Niagara*) and *There's No Business Like Show Business*, a musical featuring Marilyn as a stage performer. She also made headlines when she was suspended by Fox for her repeated failure to appear on the set for filming, a tardiness she would later explain away by claiming, "I am invariably late for appointments - sometimes as much as two hours. I've tried to change my ways but the things that make me late are too strong, and too pleasing." Of course, being a big star afforded her the leeway that she could never have gotten away with years earlier.

Nevertheless, Marilyn made more headlines outside of the studio. In January 1954, she married baseball star Joe DiMaggio and went on a honeymoon with him to Tokyo. After their honeymoon, she and DiMaggio visited the American troops in Korea, where Marilyn performed before a crowded throng of soldiers. This performance had a lasting impact on Marilyn's career; she had always despised performing before live audiences and was prone to severe bouts of stage fright. Her habit of stuttering could be covered up when acting in films, since the director could simply reshoot a take in which she stuttered, but she was not afforded this luxury when performing live. However, her performance was a success, and she credited it with giving her added confidence in later films.

Appearing before the troops in February 1954

Ironically, Marilyn's marriage with the famous Bronx Bomber was doomed from the start because of his shy and insecure nature. Put simply, DiMaggio failed to offer Marilyn the affection that she needed, and he was also abusive towards her. The couple would divorce in October, after less than a year of marriage, but they would remain friends for the rest of Marilyn's life.

Joe DiMaggio and Marilyn Monroe on their honeymoon

In 1954, Marilyn signed with a new agent, Charles Feldman of the Famous Artists Agency. Her ban from Fox was lifted shortly thereafter, and she signed on to appear in a new film, *The Seven Year Itch*, released in 1955. No film is more emblematic of Marilyn than *The Seven Year Itch*, and the film incorporates every aspect of her star persona. The plot involves a man who is separated from his family for the summer. Trapped in his apartment, he is left to fantasize over a beautiful woman who lives in the apartment above him. Marilyn is typecast again, but she is viewed affectionately by the main character, as opposed to disparaging portrayals in *All About Eve*.

The film is best remembered for a scene in which Marilyn's skirt is blown upward by the wind, which infuriated DiMaggio. Although Marilyn is certainly glamorous in the film, *The Seven Year Itch* is a curious film because it frames glamour within the realm of everyday life. Marilyn's character is nothing more than the girl who lives in the apartment above the main character, and her ordinariness marks a stark contrast from the icy film noir femme fatales that epitomized glamour during the 1940s, or the big-budget heroines from the epic films of the 1950s. Similar to *Don't Bother to Knock*, Marilyn is portrayed as someone who is overwhelmingly beautiful while still remaining merely the girl next door. Dyer noted:

> "Monroe, so much set up in terms of sexuality, also seemed to personify naturalness. Her perceived naturalness not only guaranteed the truth of her sexuality, in much the same way as imputed qualities of sincerity and authenticity, spontaneity and openness, guarantee the personality of other stars;

it was also to define and justify that sexuality".

In a sense, by tying Marilyn Monroe's natural beauty to everyday life and portraying her as a normal girl, her star image and status as a sex symbol became even more scandalous. Marilyn Monroe and the characters she played in films were certainly not the daughters conservative Americans hoped they were raising in the '50s. Films like *The Seven Year Itch* offered narratives similar to what could be found on television shows at the time, but television could not include scenes like Marilyn's white dress blowing up on the grate. Cinema provided an added attraction that television could not match.

The Seven Year Itch was Marilyn's only movie in 1955, and she would never again appear in more than one film per year. As she gained fame, she had more liberty to select the projects in which she wanted to appear, as well as the director. In February 1955, Marilyn met Lee Strasberg, the famous acting teacher in charge of the Actors Studio. Strasberg agreed for Marilyn to attend classes, and she began doing so later that year, but whether she was an active participant in the classes is still up for debate. According to James Naremore, Marilyn's attendance was little more than a mutually beneficial publicity stunt between her and Strasberg: "As for Monroe, she did little more than attend a few sessions at the Studio when she was already a star, sitting in the background and helping Strasberg become a celebrity". Meanwhile, other biographers, including Donald Spoto and Jonathan Rosenbaum, contend that Marilyn was a devoted attendee of the classes and that they influenced her later performances.

Strasberg

There's no doubt Strasberg stood to gain a great deal from having Marilyn Monroe attend his workshop, but Marilyn certainly had plenty of motivation to actively participate in the classes. Long typecast as a dumb blonde, by participating in the classes and assimilating the Method Acting practices of the Actors Studio, Marilyn had a chance to acquire respectability as an actress and distance herself from a pejorative stereotype. At a time during which she was gaining creative control over her films, she seemed to be trying to learn the kind of acting techniques that she could apply to various roles.

Marilyn's newfound authority over her career crystallized in October, when the production company she founded (Marilyn Monroe Productions) merged with 20th Century Fox, initiating a new chapter in the on-again, off-again relationship between Marilyn and that film studio. The first film in which she chose to appear was *Bus Stop* (1956), an adaptation of a Broadway play directed by Joshua Logan. It is no accident that Marilyn chose to act in an adaptation of a play, because the Actors Studio privileged a form of acting predicated on protracted scenes, which are far more common in theater. The film featured Marilyn as a woman involved in a tumultuous relationship with a young cowboy, but the plot is not as memorable as Marilyn's performance, which featured a far more emotive technique than her early films. It seems she was learning something at the Actors Studio.

Marilyn's following project, *The Prince and the Showgirl*, was also highly theatrical and featured noted actor Laurence Olivier as director. Often forgotten in discussions of Marilyn's career, the plot involves the romance between Marilyn as an American stage performer and Olivier's character, the Prince Regent of Carpathia. Set in 1911, the film appeared dated even at the time of its release and was met with lukewarm reviews.

No longer wed to DiMaggio, Marilyn became involved in another relationship during 1956, and that July she married Arthur Miller. A well-known playwright, Monroe had met Miller through her connection with the famous film director Elia Kazan. The relationship with both Kazan and Miller was made possible through her connection with the Actors Studio, since both men were good friends of Lee Strasberg. Prior to marrying Miller, Marilyn converted to Judaism and they had a Jewish wedding.

The Monroe-Miller pairing was an odd one, especially since the playwright was over 10 years older than Marilyn and a highly-regarded public intellectual. It is likely that her attraction to him was borne out of a desire to rid herself of the dumb blonde identity, which she could achieve by surrounding herself with highbrow intellectuals. The extent to which she truly loved Miller is debatable, but Marilyn's life and career trajectories reflect an increasing need to be embraced for her intellectual merits, which was more achievable through associations with figures like Miller.

Arthur Miller

1956 was a happy year for Marilyn until she suffered a miscarriage. Over the next year, her behavior became more erratic, highlighted by an increasing addiction to prescription drugs. Making matters worse, in 1957 Miller was called upon to testify before the House Committee on Un-American Activities, where he was indicted on two counts of contempt. Later in 1957, Marilyn suffered another miscarriage, just one month after learning of her pregnancy. Her behavior became increasingly erratic, and she acted in no films during that year.

In April 1958, Marilyn finally agreed to appear in a new film, signing on for *Some Like it Hot* (1959), arguably her most famous film. After more serious portrayals in *Bus Stop* and *The Prince and the Showgirl*, the film represented a return to the more zany plots of Marilyn's earliest films. Still, it offered her a great deal of respectability and press, not only because of the film's large budget but because Billy Wilder was a highly-regarded director. Similar to Fritz Lang, Wilder had emigrated from Germany during the Third Reich, and he was famous worldwide for directing films like the noir classic *Double Indemnity* (1944) and *Sunset Boulevard* (1950). Marilyn's co-stars were Tony Curtis and Jack Lemmon, who portray musicians accidentally caught up with the mob. To escape the mob, they join an all-girl band that features Marilyn's character, Sugar Kane. Although *Some Like it Hot* is most remembered for the cross dressing conducted by Lemmon and Curtis, it features a confident performance from Marilyn as well, and Wilder's cinematography lusts after her voluptuous figure. The film featured three musical numbers from Marilyn, including the memorable "I Wanna Be Loved By You."

Marilyn in *Some Like It Hot*

Some Like it Hot was a massive success, grossing $25 million at the box office, but Marilyn was reticent to appear in a new film. She was also depressed as a result of another miscarriage suffered in December 1958. In 1960, Marilyn began attending psychotherapy, not only because she was in a stressful profession but also because she was paranoid that she would develop dementia like her mother. Despite meeting with therapist Ralph Greenson on a daily basis, Monroe remained depressed.

Chapter 6: The End

"I don't mind making jokes, but I don't want to look like one." – Marilyn Monroe

The final film that Marilyn made for 20th Century Fox was *Let's Make Love* (1960), a romantic comedy featuring her and Yves Montand. Marilyn plays the part of Amanda Dell, a showgirl who falls in love with a billionaire (Montand) role-playing as an actor portraying himself in a production. The plot borrows loosely from *Some Like it Hot*, and Marilyn associates with someone who conceals their actual identity in both films. However, *Let's Make Love* is a less joyous film, and whether or not the script demanded for her to behave in such a manner, her character exudes an overriding sense of melancholy.

In an attempt to help her come to terms with her miscarriages, Arthur Miller wrote a film treatment that was meant to star Marilyn in an autobiographical role. Titled *The Misfits* (1961), the film was not a joyous rendering of Marilyn's life but instead depicted a group of alienated characters who join forces in Reno, Nevada. The filming was tumultuous, mostly due to Marilyn's erratic attendance, which substantially delayed the film's production and drove the other actors to frustration. During the filming, Marilyn had a nervous breakdown, and her marriage with Miller naturally suffered as well.

The autobiographical plot features Marilyn in the role of Roslyn Tabor, a divorcee who falls in love with Gay Langland, portrayed by Clark Gable. Given that the film also starred Montgomery Clift, it may seem surprising that Marilyn would become romantically involved with Gable, and this is one aspect in which the film reveals its autobiographical bent. As a child, Marilyn had long fantasized over Gable, and she was even prone to mentioning that he was her father due to his resemblance with Gifford, the man Gladys had told her was her father. The romantic pairing with Gable not only fulfilled a childhood fantasy but was also indicative of the manner in which Marilyn's husbands often took the form of father figures, a dynamic that found its way into Marilyn's real life in the form of both Arthur Miller (ten years her senior) and James Dougherty.

Perhaps as a result of the production difficulties, *The Misfits* received mixed reviews and did not perform well at the box office. It is easy to blame Marilyn's erratic behavior, but she criticized the script treatment, arguing that Miller did not know how to write for the screen. Regardless, her character is a sympathetic one, and the viewer is invited to feel her pain, an effect resulting from the lingering shots of her meeting the camera in direct address. It has also been argued that Marilyn's character in *The Misfits* is commensurate with the more ethical characters that Marilyn portrayed following her tenure with the Actors Studio, and this is certainly a possibility. In any case, Marilyn is portrayed sympathetically, despite the film's somewhat demeaning title.

Marilyn in *The Misfits*, her final film

Marilyn had not planned for *The Misfits* to be her last film, and she had actually signed on to act in *Something's Gotta Give*, a film that was never completed. Set to star Marilyn and Dean Martin, the production was never able to gain momentum due to her erratic behavior. Nine days after *The Misfits* finished filming, Clark Gable died, and his wife blamed Marilyn's repeated production delays for causing his death. This left Marilyn so despondent that she actually started to contemplate suicide.

As Marilyn continued to suffer problems of all kinds, it became clear that the marriage with Arthur Miller was unsustainable, and the two got a quick divorce in late January 1961. She was then hospitalized at the Payne Whitney Psychiatric Clinic in February, and she subsequently moved to the less restrictive Columbia Presbyterian Hospital at DiMaggio's urging.

After being released from the hospital, Marilyn resumed her normal activities, which included planning for *Something's Gotta Give* and an active social life. Late in 1961, Marilyn was introduced to President John F. Kennedy and his brother, Attorney General Robert F. Kennedy, through friend Peter Lawford.

Marilyn with the Kennedy brothers

Marilyn's relationships with Bobby and John Kennedy are the most dissected relationships of her life, and certainly the most controversial. It was no secret that she and the president had an affair after they met; the only debate was over the extent of it. She would later sing "Happy Birthday" for a celebration of President Kennedy's 45th birthday in 1962, wearing a tight-fitting dress and singing in such a sultry manner that Kennedy jokingly thanked her and said, "I can now retire from politics after having had Happy Birthday sung to me in such a sweet, wholesome way." Descriptions of the affair between Marilyn and the president range from a very typical extramarital affair to versions that depict Marilyn as obsessed and in love. One of Kennedy's other mistresses claimed that Marilyn constantly called the White House and entertained fantasies about marrying the president. When Kennedy broke off the affair, Marilyn was allegedly despondent and on the verge of suicide yet again.

Marilyn singing "Happy Birthday, Mr. President"

Early in 1962, Marilyn moved into a new home, hiring her close confidant, Eunice Murray, as housekeeper. Filming for *Something's Gotta Give* began in April, but Marilyn's attendance was so spotty that she was fired in June. Later that summer, she posed for a series of magazine shoots, appearing for *Vogue* and *Cosmopolitan*.

Marilyn in 1962

Marilyn grew increasingly dependent on prescription drugs, including a potent mix of Nembutal and chloral hydrate. Late at night on October 4, 1962, Marilyn Monroe was found dead in her room by Eunice.

Marilyn may have been controversial in life, but her death is still one of the most talked about mysteries of the 20th century. The exact cause of her death is unclear and has provoked a wide array of logical conclusions and conspiracy theories. The facts are murky, and various people who talked to her or saw her during the day provided different details about her mental state. While Joe DiMaggio Jr. said that Marilyn sounded upbeat on the phone around 7:00 p.m., that night, Peter Lawford claimed she sounded groggy and her speech was slurred around 7:30.

Lawford also claimed that she told him, "Say goodbye to Jack…say goodbye to yourself."

Marilyn's death was originally classified as a barbiturates overdose, but certain evidence suggested this was not the case, including the fact that there was no vomit at the scene. Although the toxicology report found levels of Nembutal and chloral hydrate that were high enough to kill 10 people, pathologist Dr. Thomas Noguchi claimed he didn't find Nembutal in her stomach, suggesting that she hadn't swallowed the drugs that killed her. The levels found in the toxicology report would have required swallowing upwards of 50-90 pills, but the examination of her body also found no evidence that the drugs had been taken through an IV. Other evidence, including photographs, was lost.

The most famous conspiracy theory has revolved around the belief that Marilyn was the victim of a murder plot involving the Kennedys and mutual friend Peter Lawford. Given that it implicates people at the highest reaches of government and involves two of the most famous men of the 20th century, it's no surprise that the Kennedy brothers are frequently tied to her death. One FBI document written at the time stated that Marilyn had threatened to make her affair with Kennedy public after he had promised to divorce Jackie and ultimately didn't. The Kennedy conspiracy theory thus asserts that the President and/or his brother sought to silence her by having her killed.

However, a more recent theory suggests that Marilyn died from a lethal combination of Nembutal and chloral hydrate, and that Marilyn was murdered not by the Kennedys but rather killed intentionally or accidentally by Dr. Greenson (who had prescribed the Nembutal) and Dr. Hyman Engelberg (who issued the chloral hydrate). Because the two doctor were close friends, one biographer has argued that they had to have known they were administering drugs that were lethal when taken in conjunction. While this theory seems plausible, no motive is proffered to explain why the doctors would kill her.

Marilyn Monroe's life is steeped in paradox. On the one hand, she lived the last decade of her life in the public eye, but her life and death are shrouded in mystery. She possessed a figure that millions of Americans would love to have, but she resented her body for failing to produce the children that she wanted to raise. Her fame brought her as far as possible from her impoverished upbringing, but she was ultimately unable to escape the mental illness that had stricken her mother. All of this has helped form the basis for Marilyn's enduring mystique as an example of the difficulties involved in being a celebrity.

As a result of her complex star image, Marilyn's legacy has been interpreted in many ways. The film critic Pauline Kael argues that Marilyn was a forerunner of the ironic glamour that typified the style of Andy Warhol. Such irony is not evident in her films, with the possible exception of *Gentlemen Prefer Blondes*, and Kael's viewpoint likely refers to Marilyn's cultural reception. At any rate, the ironic reading of Marilyn led to her appropriation as both a camp and gay icon.

What has struck many is the way in which Marilyn's bubbly and ditzy roles were at such odds with her life, particularly her turbulent final years. The end result saddened a lot of people, as did the way in which Marilyn became both conflated with her archetype and still viewed as the troubled celebrity who had something inherently wrong with her. As writer Thomas Pynchon put it in 1965, "When Marilyn Monroe got out of the game, I wrote something like, 'Southern California's special horror notwithstanding, if the world offered nothing, nowhere to support or make bearable whatever her private grief was, then it is that world, and not she, that is at fault.' I wrote that in the first few shook-up minutes after hearing the bulletin sandwiched in between Don and Phil Everly and surrounded by all manner of whoops and whistles coming out of an audio signal generator, like you are apt to hear on the provincial radio these days. But I don't think I'd take those words back."

Of course, despite all the issues and intrigue, Marilyn is best remembered today as one of the 20th century's greatest pop culture fixtures. She was instrumental in pushing sexuality to the forefront of society and reshaping American culture in the process. Her characters were a response to the conservative 1950s, the "least adult decade in movie, and national, history," and she ushered in a more liberal and relaxed view toward sexuality as a whole. All of the academic disciplines falling under the umbrella category of Cultural Studies owe a debt of gratitude to Marilyn, and though she died prematurely, her impact on culture will ensure that she remains just as famous in the future as she was in her heyday.

Jayne Mansfield

Chapter 1: Young Bride

"My father was the only man I ever knew who really loved me unselfishly, who never used me for personal gain." – Jayne Mansfield

Vera Jayne Palmer was born on April 19, 1933 in Bryn Mawr, Pennsylvania. Her father, Herbert William Palmer, was descended from German immigrants and a successful attorney. Not long after Jayne was born, the family moved to Phillipsburg, New Jersey, where he joined the practice of Robert B. Meyner, who would later become the governor of the State of New Jersey. Jayne's mother, Vera Jeffrey Palmer, had grown up in Pennsylvania in a wealthy industrialist family.

Jayne would be her parents' only child, and she later recalled, "Mama had lost a little boy through natural birth, so it was decided that I would be a Caesarean. I always knew I was wanted because Mama wouldn't have taken such a personal risk if she didn't want me. In those days doctors didn't recommend any more pregnancies after a C-section."

Tragically, Herbert died of a heart attack when Jayne was only three years old, and he was driving a car at the time with Vera and Jayne as passengers: "We were driving up a steep hill.

We were all laughing and joking. Mama thought of something funny about a dinner party she was giving that night. She started to tell Daddy about it. Suddenly our laughter froze. Daddy fell over against Mama. He was dead. Just like that. My daddy was gone. It started to rain, and there we were, mama and me and the rain washing away our tears. The rain has been my tormentor. All my life."

Now a widow with a young daughter to support, Vera taught for a few years in the Phillipsburg School System, but even though times were tight, she and her daughter never missed a Shirley Temple movie. Vera told one woman, "I used to promise her if she was a good little girl we'd go to the movies and she could have chewing gum, lollipops and ice cream. And you know, I might have instilled something in her at that tender age." Like most young girls growing up in the 1930s, Jayne was fascinated by Temple and dreamed of being a movie star like her: "I came home and imitated the stars in some of the scenes. I knew then I was going to be a movie star someday. When Mama saw me acting in front of the mirror in the bedroom I told her that I was going to be a movie star."

Shirley Temple in 1933

In 1939, Vera married Harry Lawrence Peers, and the family moved to Dallas, Texas. Though Peers did not formally adopt Jayne, she nonetheless referred to herself as Jayne Peers after they moved to Texas. When she was 12, she persuaded Vera to let her take ballroom dancing classes, but unlike the tap dancing that Temple did for entertainment, Jayne's ballroom dancing was designed to help her fit into Dallas society. The same was true of her music lessons in viola, violin and piano.

Jayne was a good student at Highland Park High School and later claimed to have an I.Q. of 163. She enjoyed studying languages and became fluent in German and Spanish during high school. She would later master French and Italian, leading one reporter to later dub her the "smartest dumb blond" in Hollywood. When asked about her intellect, Jayne would always reply knowingly, "They're more interested in 40-21-35." Still, Jayne might have gone on to significant academic success had she not also majored in boys in high school. At a Christmas party during her senior year, she met a young man named Paul James Mansfield, and recalling their first meeting, she said, "It was the most conservative Christmas Eve I ever spent. He was not a great talker. He had a silent way of moving and taking over. I liked that and I was enveloped by his subtle masculinity. I don't mean sexually. I mean the firmness with which he handled himself. I respected him."

Mansfield was a handsome, popular young man, and the two soon became an item before secretly marrying on January 28, 1950. Paul would later recall, "I began calling her and then we began dating. I felt really proud when we walked down the street with this gorgeous thing on my arm. Late January we just decided to elope. We didn't tell anybody about it. She was sixteen, I was twenty, twenty-one. I was young and in love and she was too. We got married in a fever, hotter than a couple of cats." Not long after their elopement, Jayne learned she was pregnant, after which the two then told their parents. Their parents, believing they were not yet married, arranged a small ceremony on May 10, just weeks before Jayne graduated from high school. Their daughter, Jayne Marie Mansfield, was born six months later, on November 8, 1950.

In spite of their early marriage, Paul and Jayne were determined to go on with their educations. In the fall of 1950, Paul enrolled in Southern Methodist University as an acting major, and after Jayne Marie was born, Jayne joined him in school, bringing the baby with her to classes. Later in 1951, the two moved to Austin, where they studied drama at the University of Texas. Jayne remembered, "I did Jayne Marie's laundry in the bathtub, and I cooked and cleaned, too, just like any young wife. And it didn't hurt my marks either. I even got an A in chemistry." To make ends meet, Jayne took jobs selling books, working as a dance studio receptionist, and also as a nude model for some of the college's art classes: "I found I could pose in the nude in front of a women's sculpturing class without any embarrassment, or even a feeling of uneasiness. Soon after that a men's sculpturing class asked me to pose for them. They even offered to up the price, but that I didn't like."

Jayne stayed busy with extracurricular activities within the school as well. She joined the university's Curtain Club, where she met future stars Tom Jones and Rip Torn, and she also did some acting at the Austin Civic Theater. Anxious to make a name for herself, Jayne entered and won a number of beauty pageants around Austin, earning the titles of Miss Magnesium Lamp, Miss Photoflash, and Miss Fire Prevention Week, though she rejected that of Miss Roquefort Cheese because it "just didn't sound right." Among the other titles were Gas Station Queen, Miss Third Platoon, Miss Blues Bonnet of Austin, Cherry Blossom Queen, Miss Direct Mail, Miss Analgesic, Miss Electric Switch, Miss Negligee, Nylon Sweater Queen, Miss Fill-er-up, Miss One for the Road, Hot Dog Ambassador, Miss Freeway, Miss Geiger Counter, Best Dressed Woman of Theater, Miss 100% Pure Maple Syrup, Miss Texas Tomato, Miss July Fourth, Miss Standard Foods, Miss Potato Soup, Miss Orchid, Miss Lobster, Miss Chihuahua Show and Miss United Dairies.

The Mansfield's moved back to Dallas in 1952, and Jayne was able to study for a while with the famous actor Baruch Lumet, whose son, Sidney, would also become famous in the entertainment world, but as a director. Jayne and Paul both continued to take part in the local theater scene, with Jayne's mother babysitting in while they worked on shows like *Ten Nights in a Barroom* and *The Slaves of Demon Rum*. Later in the year, however, Paul was drafted and the two moved to Camp Gordon, Georgia, where they would remain there while Paul served in the U.S. Army Reserve. They would also continue acting in their spare time, including appearing in a local production of *Anything Goes*.

When Paul was sent to Korea, Jayne returned to Dallas and picked up where she had left off, appearing with Lumet in *Death of a Salesman* on October 22, 1953. This production, staged at the Knox Street Theater, was her biggest role to date and earned her an audition with Paramount Pictures. Lumet helped prepare Jayne for her audition, but she did not get a contract with Paramount. She then auditioned for Warner Brothers' next big movie, *The Seven Year Itch*, but she couldn't land a role in that picture either. After auditioning for a role in *Joan of Arc* for Paramount, Jayne finally landed her first role in *An Angel Went AWOL*, a televised production for CBS' Lux Video Theatre. Mainly cast as eye candy, she only had a few lines and spent most of her onstage time in a sultry pose on top of a piano. She earned $300 for her work.

Chapter 2: Aspiring Actress

"To establish yourself as an actress, you have to become well known. A girl just starting out, I would tell her to concentrate on acting, but she doesn't have to go around wearing blankets." – Jayne Mansfield

By the time Paul returned home from Korea, his wife had been thoroughly bitten by the acting bug, so the young couple decided to leave little Jayne Marie in Dallas with her grandparents and move to Los Angeles. According to Paul, "I saw the Los Angeles area as a good area as any to establish myself too. And I was willing to take her there and look for work myself. She changed her hair to blonde; they liked blondes back then. She was getting better looking every day, you know, and I was playing my role. I told her that I would take her to California and I would standby and give her her opportunity."

Paul took a job with a local newspaper, and Jayne enrolled at UCLA. She also began indulging her love of pets, opening their home to three cats, two Chihuahuas, a rabbit, a Great Dane and a poodle which she dyed her signature color pink. She would later admit that she had wanted to choose purple, but lavender was already associated with actress Kim Novak: "It must have been the right decision because I got more column space from pink than Kim Novak ever did from lavender." On April 30, 1954, she went to Paramount Studios and told anyone who would listen, "I want to be an actress. I have modeled and won many beauty contests. What do I do?"

Kim Novak in *Vertigo* **(1958)**

Jayne came to Hollywood at the perfect time for someone with her looks and physical attributes. When she and Paul managed to make it out to see a movie, they sometimes saw something starring Columbia Pictures' newest sensation, Marilyn Monroe. She was taking the country by storm, but there was only one of her, so every other studio in the city was looking for their own version. Fox had tried grooming a number of actresses into being the new Marilyn, and one of them, June Haver, had looked like she might be their answer until she left the studio in 1953 to become a nun. Another, Sheree North, was too independent to be molded into someone else. Monroe would long consider Mansfield a rival and complain about the way Jayne was using her image, telling one reporter, ""All she does is imitate me--but her imitations are an insult to her as well as to myself. I know it's supposed to be flattering to be imitated, but she does it so grossly, so vulgarly - I wish I had some legal means to sue her."

Monroe

In the meantime, according to one historian, "The American economy soared even higher, and the tailfins on cars swelled, along with women's busts and bouffant hairdos. The time was ripe for the Blonde as Bombshell, a new, over-the-top, va-va-voom icon. She arrived in the form of Jayne Mansfield." In the end, Jayne's passion for acting would be her undoing. There were actresses who became respected professionals, but they had to wait and work and choose their parts carefully. Young Jayne did not have the patience; she was in a hurry for fame and was willing to do whatever it took to get it, so she went the path of least resistance and began to play the "dumb blond." Still, those closest to her would always know the truth. As an adult, her daughter Jayne Marie would observe, "It was an act; the whole thing was an act. She was a concert violinist and pianist and she spoke five languages. I think she was misunderstood, but it was her own doing. I mean she was the one that walked in there and said, 'this is what I want' and 'I'll take it' and 'I'll do it', not realizing the consequences." Jayne Marie later added, "Unfortunately the first role that pivoted her up to semi-stardom was that of a dumb blonde. And I think that that unfortunately, down the line, was the downfall. Because you're talking of an era that ended pretty quickly."

Though Paramount tested her for a role in *Joan of Arc*, they were not impressed. Still, Jayne remained undeterred: "So on a bright Tuesday morning, I got on a bus to go to the nearest studio to my home, Republic Studios. In the casting office it was all routine. Name, address, height, experience. I was one of several other young girls, some of them very pretty, in fact prettier than I was. It was a shock. It was a pretty discouraging session. From there I went to Universal Studios where I went through the same experience. At Warner Brothers, my next stop, they had certain hours for interviewing talent and I was there at the wrong time."

Jayne finally won a small part in *Female Jungle*. Her first supporting role, it earned her $150 but very little attention. Still, Jayne would recall, "I loved seeing me up there on the screen. I was filled with a chill. I had finally made it and wanted to stay there. 'I love you Jayne Mansfield,' I told my image. 'I'll work hard for you! Nothing or no one could ever make me let you down.'"

Determined, Jayne visited James Byron, a well-known Hollywood publicist, on Christmas Eve 1954. Handing him a wrapped gift, she smiled her most winning smile and asked him to represent her. Taking in the platinum blond hair and her famous 40-21-35 figure, he agreed, and according to one Hollywood insider, this was all part of a bigger plan for the shrewd business man. "He signed twenty or thirty girls and hoped one of them was gonna make it. And that'll help him. So he signed them all for five percent of their gross. And she was one of the girls."

Byron went to work right away, arranging for her to fly down to Florida, where Jane Russell was filming *Underwater* for RKO. Byron arranged for a group of reporters to interview her poolside, and she showed up wearing a much too small red bikini. With a big smile at the photographers around her, she dove into the pool, only to emerge blushing and giggling when her top "mysteriously" fell off. Jayne would later tell this story, adding, "It wasn't even my own costume. I borrowed it from Peter Gowland, the still photographer, who kept it in his studio for models. It was red lame and skin tight, it covered everything but didn't hide anything. When I took off my robe…I thought I'd forgotten to put it on."

Needless to say, she got their attention, and that of much of the entertainment world. The following month, Warner Brothers offered her a 7 year contract for $250 a week.

Chapter 3: Playgirl

"A forty-one inch bust and a lot of perseverance will get you more than a cup of coffee-a lot more. But most girls don't know what to do with what they've got."- Jayne Mansfield

In addition to getting a contract with Warner Brothers that February, Jayne also made her first appearance in the relatively new but very popular *Playboy* magazine. The issue was a success for both her and the publication, and she went on to appear nude for that year's *Playboy* calendar. She would be the Valentine's Day girl for four of the next five years.

Obviously, her appearance in *Playboy* sparked a good deal of conversation about her body, specifically her measurements. In fact, famous evangelist Billy Graham would complain during this time, "This country knows more about Jayne Mansfield's statistics than the Second Commandment." However, this wasn't entirely true, because few could agree on exactly what those statistics were. In 1955, she claimed a 22-inch waist and a 41 inch bust, but as the years passed, and her body went through the changes of five pregnancies, those numbers would also change. By the time she died, her cup size was up to 46DD, and her chest, along with that of other similarly endowed starlets, had been credited with the development of the 1950s style brassiere.

It came as a surprise to few when Jayne filed for divorce shortly after her appearance in *Playboy*, since being a wife just did not go along with her new image. Neither did her stunts, pets and cheating, as Paul explained, "I had begun not to like what I saw and I told her that. I just couldn't stand the attention she was receiving from other men, I didn't know how we were going to take care of little Jayne Marie in a family kind of atmosphere with that going on. Of course you could say that my leaving didn't help that, but still it seemed wrong to me so I chose to tell her that. I could see myself as a Mr. Jaynie Mansfield and that really wasn't what I had sought for my life. So along about the spring of 1955 we separated and took a job in San Francisco and moved away." Of course, Jayne disagreed, saying, "I read little Bible stories to Jayne Marie every night and she is a well-balanced and intelligent child. Those pictures in *Playboy* magazine I posed for to get milk and bread for the baby."

The contrast between Jayne the sex symbol and Jane the mother would remain an interesting twist for the rest of Jayne's life. It was hard for 1950s Hollywood to accept that the same woman who said "I love sex... It should be animalistic, it should be sadistic, it should at times be masochistic... There are few rules and moral conventions" also said, "Carrying a baby is the most rewarding experience a woman can enjoy." As one writer put it, "It was a contrast—the shapely Jayne in her sex-symbol clothes snuggling the child on her lap in affectionate, motherly poses. This was unique. It aroused even greater interest than Jayne photographed with men she dated."

Jayne and Paul would spend the next two years involved in a very messy divorce that probably helped Jayne's career by drawing even more attention to her antics, including the two times on June 8, 1955 when the dress she was wearing suddenly fell to her waist, both times in very public places. The headlines generated during this time also probably ensured she kept the name Jayne Mansfield professionally for the rest of her life.

During 1955, Jayne played small parts in several Warner Brothers films, including *Pete Kelly's Blues* (with Jack Webb) and *Hell on Frisco*, starring Alan Ladd. Her biggest small role was with Edward G. Robinson in *Illegal*, which earned her first mention in a movie review, and her first written comparison to Marilyn Monroe at that. Famous film critic Bosley Crowther observed, "*Illegal* tries to blueprint *The Asphalt Jungle's* Marilyn Monroe. You may remember that Miss

Monroe's first screen role was in the latter. She spoke not a word but she went right to work as an adornment in the apartment of the criminal counselor. Well, in *Illegal* Jayne Mansfield plays precisely the same sort of role in the apartment of Albert Dekker, the big poobah of crime. Miss Mansfield, we might add, is the beauty who is imitating Miss Monroe in a feeble imitation of *Once In a Lifetime* on the Broadway stage."

As Crowther mentioned, by the time *Illegal* was released, Mansfield had decided she no longer wanted her Warner Brothers contract, and with the help of James Byron, she hired lawyer Greg Bautzer to get her out of it. She then moved on to Broadway, where her new agent, William Shiffrin, had secured her first major role in the musical spoof, *Will Success Spoil Rock Hunter?* Appearing opposite Walter Matthau and Orson Bean, Mansfield starred as a Marilyn Monroe-esque character named Rita Marlowe. Her main costume for the play was a skimpy bath towel, leading one critic to praise the "commendable abandon" in which she played "a platinum-pated movie siren with the wavy contours of Marilyn Monroe". The show ran 450 performances, making Mansfield a legend in the world of Hollywood to Broadway transitions.

Determined to make the most of her new role, Mansfield did her own publicity work: "Almost every store window in New York City had my picture in front, and those that didn't – I would go in personally and hand them one. Then I got the idea of blow-ups, five-feet-by-three. I'd autograph them to a respective shop or store and walk in with one and give it to the owner. I had many different poses, so each would have an exclusive. No one refused me. And there I was, block after block, smiling out at the public."

In May 1956, Jayne left New York to return to Hollywood, bringing a new $20,000 mink coat with her, and within days of her return, she had a new six-year contract with 20ᵗʰ Century Fox. Over the next few months she would divide her time on the east and west coasts as she continued to play her role in *Rock Hunter,* winning a Theatre World Award for Promising Personality for her work. For her part, Mansfield loved the role of Rita Marlowe, saying, "She is brassy and extroverted, refreshing and direct and not entirely oblivious of her bombshell of a body. The role gives me a chance to act on stage the way I would like to behave offstage."

For nine months beginning in September 1956, Mansfield's photo was featured in newspapers more than 2,500 times, and many of these photos and mentions related to yet another publicity stunt she pulled in April 1957. While attending a dinner party in honor of Italian actress Sophia Loren, Mansfield bent so far over the table that one of her large breasts "accidentally" fell out of the top of her dress. She later claimed, "I really had no idea so much of me was showing. I only realized when I saw the expression on Miss Loren's face and I noticed that she was staring down my dress. Some enemies said I planned the strategy to take the play away from Miss Loren. Not at all. Though I did show Miss Loren that American girls have bosoms too."

Loren

While many papers covered the story and published the photos, most touched up the photo to cover Mansfield's nipple. With so much attention, she was quickly becoming one of the most notorious actresses in Hollywood.

Mansfield with actor Steve Cochran and Ed Wynne, the owner of the Harwyn Club in New York. This picture was taken at the Harwyn Club.

"Sex appeal is a wonderful, warm, womanly, healthy feeling. If you're a woman it's womanly, if you're not its manly...it comes only from inside...it's an effervescent desire to enjoy life." – Jayne Mansfield

The public attention and her work on Broadway earned Mansfield a starring role in *The Girl Can't Help It* in 1956. This was one of the earliest rock and roll musicals made, and it featured several popular rock stars of the day, including Fats Domino and Little Richard. She worked on the picture while still working on *Rock Hunter*, but she did so well in the movie that Fox bought out her contract, effectively shutting *Rock Hunter* down. They then began billing Jayne Mansfield as "Marilyn Monroe king-sized." Her co-star, Tony Randall, praised her, saying, "At least she tried to be a professional. She would show up and rehearse and work and shoot it. She had a sense of humor about her."

During the time Jayne was working on *Rock Hunter*, Paul Mansfield had become increasingly disturbed about the toll her career was taking on their five year old daughter. In August, he filed for custody of the little girl but never received it. Jayne Marie would live with her mother, often traveling with her around the country and around the world, until well into her teens.

During this time, Mansfield also made her first TV appearance, playing a lead on "The Bachelor," a popular show and part of NBC's Sunday Spectacular lineup. She also did a Shakespearean recitation on a British show in 1957 and expanded her performance to include performances on the violin and piano. She guest starred on *The Bob Hope Show* three times and toured with his USO troupe for 16 days, and she also appeared on *The Ed Sullivan Show*, again playing the violin. Afterwards she told reporters, "Now I am really national. Momma and Dallas see *The Ed Sullivan Show*!" By 1958, she was so popular that she was making $20,000 per television appearance.

Mansfield and Bob Hope doing a USO show in 1957

That same year, her first dramatic film, *The Burglar*, was released by Columbia Pictures. She had actually filmed it two year earlier, just before she started work on *Rock Hunter*, and this was also producer Louis W. Kellman's first big successful movie, leading him to later claim that he was the man who discovered Jayne Mansfield. Next, Mansfield appeared in *The Wayward Bus*, based on the John Steinbeck novel of the same name. Again, she did well in this dramatic role and won a Golden Globe for New Star of the Year (Actress) in 1957. Critics "generally conceded [the film] to have been her best acting" and praised her "soft-voiced coo punctuated with squeals".

Without a doubt, Mansfield's most important movie of this era was the film version of *Will Success Spoil Rock Hunter?* in 1957. It was also the first film she made with future husband, the Hungarian born actor Miklós Hargitay. The two had met in New York in the summer of 1956, when Hargitay was still married to his first wife, Mary. Hargitay divorced Mary later that year, and Jayne divorced Paul in California in October 1956. The two began dating seriously even while Paul Mansfield was still in the process of divorcing Jayne in Texas in March of the following year, and it would be nearly another year before all the papers were finally completed on January 8, 1958. Still Jayne was determined to have what she wanted. "I knew I wanted Mickey ten minutes after we were introduced at the Latin Quarter. We have been close since. I've had to go it alone, with my family and Paul putting obstacles in my path all the way. Mickey wants to devote himself to helping my career."

Mansfield in the film version of *Will Success Spoil Rock Hunter?* **(1957)**

Hargitay

Meanwhile, in 1957, Jayne's maternal grandfather died and left her $90,000, money she used to purchase a 40-room mansion in Beverly Hills. Located on the famous Sunset Boulevard, the house soon became famous for its pink exterior, complete with cupids and pink lights, as well as pink bathrooms featuring pink fur rugs and even a heart-shaped pink bathtub. The centerpiece of the home's interior was a fountain that often shot pink champagne into the air during parties. By the time she was finished, she her estate would feature:

> A heart shaped swimming pool that said "I Love You Jaynie" on the bottom in two foot high gold mosaic tiles.

Eight bedrooms.

13 baths.

A grand scaled Pink Mink living room.

Heart shaped bed and fireplace.

A Pink Cadillac (given to her by Mickey after the birth of their son Miklos).

A Pink Jaguar.

An Eldorado Cadillac.

A closet full of minks (white, pink and black).

Twice weekly baths in Pink Champagne

A picture of the gate entrance to Mansfield's former home, the "Pink Palace".

Banking on the success of *Rock Hunter*, Fox sent Mansfield on a 40 day European tour to promote the movie, and after she attended the movie's London opening, she had the privilege of meeting England's young Queen Elizabeth II. The British people liked her, as did their movie critics, with one observing, "She had been as good an actress as her bubble-and-squeak roles have permitted her to be. The lady is friendly, the lady is warm-hearted, the lady is always good for a laugh. She is also one of the most pleasing bits of scenery in the whole pulchritudinous landscape of show business." Of course, Mansfield was working hard to become what the studio wanted her to be: the new Marilyn Monroe. She started speaking in the soft, breathy voice Monroe made famous, and she even appeared in two plays based on Monroe movies, *Bus Stop* and *Gentlemen Prefer Blondes*.

When Mansfield returned home to Hollywood, she made a guest appearance on *The Perry Como Show Holiday in Las Vegas Special,* apparently offending the audience with one of her more risqué style nightclub acts. A few days later, Hargitay had a surprise for her. He proposed in November 1957, presenting her with a $5,000 multi-carat diamond ring. While they were engaged, Mansfield starred opposite Cary Grant in *Kiss Them for Me*, but critics hated the film, calling it everything from "vapid" to "no good." Her participation in the film was a serious setback for Mansfield's career, though she made one more movie in early 1958, *The Sheriff of Fractured Jaw*. In this spoof of classic westerns, she starred opposite Kenneth More, and she was supposed to sing in it but her voice was not good enough, so her parts had to be dubbed in by Connie Francis. It would not be released until 1959, and it would wind up being her last successful mainstream film.

Mansfield in *The Sheriff of Fractured Jaw*

Chapter 5: Mansfield and Hargitay

Mansfield and Hargitay dancing at the Candy Stik Lounge in 1962.

"I have always considered my career self and my personal self as two different and separate people. There's a Jayne Mansfield at home, a wife and devoted mother, and there's Jayne the sex symbol, which is my career. I have always kept them completely apart and separate." – Jayne Mansfield

Mansfield and Hargitay were married as soon as Jayne's divorce was finalized in January 1958, but not everyone was happy with her proposed marriage. In particular, Fox was against her being tied down to one man, as it was out of keeping with the image they had worked so hard to build. But this time Jayne was adamant, saying "I know the studio doesn't want me to marry Mickey, but I'm too much woman. I've already told the studio my decision. They were gracious about it. But I don't blame Fox for being bitterly disappointed. I would be too—if I had a Jayne on my hands."

For her second wedding, Mansfield wore a form fitting pink lace gown with a 30 yard pink tulle flounce at the bottom. The two also drank pink champagne at the reception after a wedding one reporter described as having "all the hoopla of a Fourth of July picnic." "Some 1,500 fans…screamed and shouted outside the Wayfarers' Chapel during the most tender moments of the nondenominational rites. Someone even bounced a rock off the top of the all-glass church while photographers, who nearly outnumbered guests, kept banging their cameras against the glass walls."

Mansfield tried to claim that she just wanted a small, private affair, but her normal level of attention-grabbing behavior and her choice of one the most famous chapels in Hollywood, not to mention one with a glass ceiling and glass walls, make that statement pretty unbelievable. Of course, the real smoking gun of this fabrication came in the form of thousands of pink wedding announcements that Mansfield had printed up and dropped by helicopter all over Hollywood.

True to form, marriage did nothing to dampen Mansfield's desire to shock people. In fact, Hargitay was just as hungry for attention as she was, and the two soon began to cook up stunts together. The following month, while she and Hargitay were in Rio de Janeiro for Mardi Gras, she appeared at a party naked from the waist up. Then, while they were attending a West Berlin film festival, he lifted her up over his head so she could bite into the grapes hanging over the table. Once more, Mansfield "fell out" of her dress right in front of a group of photographers. The photos made headlines all over the world, with a "censored" sign placed over her most prominent features, but by now, the world was beginning to grow tired of the antics. One reporter wrote, "We are amused when Miss Mansfield strains to pull in her stomach to fill out her bikini better; but we get angry when career-seeking women, shady ladies, and certain starlets and actresses...use every opportunity to display their anatomy unasked".

In February 1958, Mansfield and Hargitay also launched their first Las Vegas show, with Mansfield appearing in a striptease revue at the Tropicana. Part of the production involved Hargitay whirling Mansfield, costumed in a gold mesh dress with a few well-placed sequins, around his waist. This portion of the act was considered so dangerous that the couple took out a special million dollar insurance policy with the famous Lloyd's of London to cover any losses resulting from him dropping her. The opening night was a fundraiser for the March of Dimes, one of Mansfield's favorite charities, and it raised over $20,000. She was paid $25,000 a week to appear in the show, which was extended from four to eight weeks. This was 10 times what Fox was paying her, and Las Vegas might have wanted to extend the revue even longer, but it would not be possible. By April 1958, Mansfield was pregnant with her second child.

A promotional poster featuring Jayne

Unfortunately, Mansfield's second pregnancy would not be a peaceful time in her life. In September 1958, Hargitay's first wife, Mary, asked for more child support for their daughter Tina, and the press turned vicious when Mansfield and Hargitay claimed that they were too poor to pay more. After all, Hargitay, a former plumber and bricklayer, had just built a beautiful heart-shaped swimming pool in their backyard, and Mansfield's Vegas salary alone was $200,000. Even still, Mansfield tried to say that they were so poor that they could not afford furniture and that she herself slept on the floor; they never mentioned the thousands of dollars of free furnishings they had received from furniture companies wanting publicity. Fortunately, all the world loves a baby, and the birth of Miklós Jeffrey Palmer Hargitay on December, 21 1958 brought her back into the public's good graces.

As soon as she recovered from Miklós's birth, Mansfield wanted to go back to work, but she soon learned that there would be no major movies coming her way. Fox was tired of dealing with her public shenanigans and poor performances, but the company's president, Spyros Skouras, was not one to turn his back on people. Jayne appreciated this, saying "Mr. Skouras was the only man I ever really respected in my life. He was as firm as any father and a real gentleman. He was a very straightforward person. He was honest enough to bluntly state his convictions. Too honest, maybe." Instead, Fox decided to loan her out to an English studio, and while overseas, she made two gangster movies. The first, *Too Hot to Handle*, marked her first step down a long path of increasingly bad movies. It claimed to be "an exposé of 'sexy, sordid Soho, England's greatest shame,'" but it was really little more than Mansfield parading around on screen in a series of transparent costumes. When the movie was finally released in America in 1961, some of the scenes actually made the cover of *Playboy* magazine. The other film, *The Challenge*, would not be released in the United States until 1963. Still, Mansfield received her star on the Hollywood Walk of Fame in February 1960.

A trailer shot of Mansfield in *Too Hot To Handle*

Mansfield's Hollywood Star

When Mansfield was offered the lead in *The Loves of Hercules*, she agreed to take it only if Hargitay could play the title role. Fox agreed to let her make the picture, knowing that she was already four months pregnant with her fourth child and thus would not be able to work much longer. The Italian movie company making the film paid Mansfield $75,000 for her appearance in the film, and though it was not a critical hit, it did develop a following in Italy. Back at home, on Mother's Day 1960, Mansfield, Hargitay and their children were named the "Family of the Year" by the Mildred Strauss Child Care Chapter of Mount Sinai Hospital, New York. Zoltán Anthony Hargitay was born a few months later, on August 1, 1960.

Chapter 6: The Blonde Bombshell Explodes

"Looks don't regulate a girl's body temperature, at least not this girl's body temperature. Intelligence in a man is the keynote and no girl in her right mind is going to go shopping for a man who's handsome and husky alone." – Jayne Mansfield

Mansfield went right back to work after Zoltán's birth, starring in a supporting role in *It Happened in Athens*. The movie was filmed on location in Greece, and the plot was built around the 1960 Olympic Games. Indeed, the movie features some live footage shot of the Games during the fall of that year. The movie was meant primarily to promote up and coming actor Trax

Colton, but it fared so poorly that both he and Mansfield, who had a brief love affair, were dropped by Fox after its release.

Without a studio contract, Mansfield once more turned her attention to Las Vegas. In December 1960, she and Hargitay opened at the Dunes Hotel and Casino in *The House of Love*. Financially, this was the high point of their career, as she earned $35,000 a week. She also made personal appearances for $10,000 a piece, opening drug stores and cutting the ribbons on supermarkets. Hargitay was also paid well, so the two were able to live very comfortably.

In 1961, Mansfield starred in yet another box-office flop, *The George Raft Story*, though in spite of her "above the title" billing, she actually had only a very small part in the movie. Looking for something else to fill her time, she made another USO tour in December 1961, this time visiting American bases in the Arctic. Once back in Hollywood, she made her first guest starring appearance on a TV show, starring in "The Dumbest Blonde" episode of *Follow the Sun*. Her role was well received and referred to by one critic as "a new and dramatic Jayne Mansfield." Mansfield also appeared in episodes of *Kraft Mystery Theater* and *Burke's Law*, as well as *Alfred Hitchcock Presents* and three episodes of *The Red Skelton Hour*. Like most fading stars of the time, she rounded out her work by appearing on games shows, showing up regularly as a panelist on *Down You Go* and a participant on *The Match Game*. She was even a mystery guest on *What's My Line?* Mansfield even released a record album during 1962; 20th Century Fox Records recorded her performance in *The House of Love* and released it as *Jayne Mansfield Busts Up Las Vegas*.

Mansfield and Barry Coe in *Follow the Sun*

Unfortunately, the world that Jayne had built her career around was changing, especially with the sudden death of Marilyn Monroe in August 1962. As one author observed, "It was strange how Marilyn's death affected the industry, and the need for blonde sex symbols. It was like all parts and work for blondes disappeared to honor her." One of these blondes, Mamie Van Doren, later explained Jayne's downfall, saying, "In all due respect to Jayne, I do not excuse myself from this near-desperate attempt to hold on to a passing style. I was trying to keep my head above the waters that were closing around us in that decade. But while I saw the end coming for us all too clearly, I don't think Jayne realized what was happening." This difference in perspective between the two women would create a very antagonistic relationship as time went on.

Mamie Van Doren in *The Navy vs. the Night Monsters* (1966)

Of course, Mansfield still figured the best way to get and hold attention was to scandalize people. In June 1962, she once again grabbed the limelight by taking off the polka-dot dress she was wearing at an Italian nightclub in Rome and dancing around the room in her undergarments. The following month, when she was awarded the Silver Mask by Italian entertainment reporters, she once again made it into the papers, though this time as a victim, after she was attacked by a woman at the ceremony and wrestled to the ground. Upon witnessing this incident, the famous Hollywood designer, Richard Blackwell, refused to work for her, saying, "I refuse to dress her anymore. I can't go on designing for an actress who shows off my work by either having the dresses ripped off her or wrestling on the floor with them. Besides, I can't stand the shoes she wears—cheap, plastic wedgies that went out long ago."

Blackwell was not the only one who'd had enough of her behavior. When Mansfield had yet another very public affair, this time with Italian producer Enrico Bomba, Hargitay became incensed and threatened to divorce her. She herself had tried half-heartedly to divorce him earlier in the year, filing papers while telling reporters, "I'm sure we will make it up." But Hargitay was serious. Her next affair, with singer Nelson Sardelli in early 1963, was the last straw, and after that, Mansfield and Hargitay flew to Mexico to complete their divorce. Sardelli went with them, supposedly as Mansfield's legal advisor. This proved to be a mistake, as the American government refused to recognize Mansfield's Mexican divorce, and she and Hargitay reconciled in October.

   Still, the affairs did not end. During her heyday as a Hollywood actress, Mansfield was
rumored to have slept with numerous men from all over the world, including the owner of the
famous Paris restaurant *Tour d'Argent,* Claude Terrail; as well as Jorge Guinle, a billionaire from
Brazil. Of course, her most famous lovers were purported to be the Kennedy brothers.
Apparently she met John F. Kennedy in Palm Springs while he was campaigning for president.
They were introduced by Peter Lawford, the president's brother-in-law and romantic broker, and
Mansfield wasn't bashful about keeping the affair private, telling one reporter, "Everyone in
Hollywood and Washington knows about it anyway, and I like it that way! And I'll bet Marilyn's
pissed as all get out!" Their affair was short lived, as she was too busy in Hollywood to spend
much time in Washington D.C. Kennedy moved on to Marilyn Monroe, and Mansfield allegedly
moved on to his brother Bobby. That affair did not last long, either, if it even happened at all.

Chapter 7: Promises! Promises!

"In the fifties, Jayne and American men had conspired to keep sex a secret. By the sixties the secret was out."

That same year, producer Tommy Noonan approached Mansfield about a very special role. He wanted her to star in *Promises! Promises!,* the first feature film length movie in the United States to contain a nude scene. George Cukor had started filming *Something's Got to Give* the previous year with Marilyn Monroe, but she had died suddenly before the movie was completed.

Unfortunately, working with Mansfield proved to be more of a challenge than Noonan had anticipated. For one thing, her marriage to Hargitay, who was also appearing in the picture, was on the rocks, and furthermore, she had a problem understanding what Noonan wanted from her. He ended up bringing in a special assistant, Jet Fore, to run interference between him and his star.

Knowing that he had only a small budget, Noonan's plan was to build the film around the three nude scenes. The first lasted almost a minute, focusing on Mansfield singing the romantic "I'm in Love" while bathing in a bubble bath. For viewers, the highlight of this scene was at the end, when the camera filmed her from behind as she bent over. The other two scenes were much shorter, lasting just seconds, but they were also more provocative. In the first, Mansfield is completely nude as she towels off. In the other, repeated multiple times throughout the movie, she is tossing and turning in bed, though at no time was the lower half of her torso visible.

As part of the publicity for the film, the producer allowed a *Playboy* photographer to photograph Mansfield on the set while filming her nude scenes, and when Hugh Hefner, the owner of the magazine, published them, he was brought up on obscenity charges in Chicago and arrested for the first and only time in his career. His trial, and the 7-5 jury vote for acquittal, only drew more attention to the movie. While Cleveland banned the film, most American cities allowed it to be shown, and though the reviews were terrible, the provocative nature of the film made it a box office hit. Its success made Mansfield one of the Top 10 Box Office Attractions that year, but as film critic Roger Ebert observed, "Finally in *Promises! Promises!* she does what no Hollywood star ever does except in desperation. She does a nudie. In 1963, that kind of box office appeal was all she had left."

Though *Promises! Promises!* may have been all Mansfield had left at the box office, she still had something to offer on the smaller screen. In November 1963, she played her violin and sang "Too Marvelous for Words" on *The Ed Sullivan Show*. She also performed different musical numbers, including *This Queen has her aces in all the right places*, *Quando-Quando*, and Marilyn Monroe's famous *Diamonds Are a Girl's Best Friend*.

Mansfield turned 30 in 1963, and as often happens during such a watershed year, she began to evaluate her personal life, and particularly her spirituality. Though she had been raised in mainstream Protestant churches, she had never had a sense of her own faith. She started to think about the impact of this missing piece and began attending Catholic masses while in Europe. Once she returned to America, she seriously toyed with the idea of becoming Catholic, though she never did. She later observed, "I guess a lot of people think that a girl who shows her bosom and wears tight dresses can't be close to God. God has always been close to me. Only He knew what was in my heart." Still, she did regularly attend mass with any Catholic man she was married to or dating, and she raised her children with second husband Mickey Hargitay in the Catholic Church. Her faith also informed her opinions on the Civil Rights movement, leading her to say, "I don't want to get involved in the racial situation at the expense of losing fans. I wouldn't say anything too strong but I do know that God created us equal and we're not living up to it."

Of course, Mansfield had other things of a less spiritual nature on her mind during the last half of 1963. She was pregnant with her fourth child, a daughter born on January 23, 1964 named Mariska Magdalena Hargitay. By this time, she had already sued the State of California, demanding that they recognize her Mexican divorce, and she and Hargitay were finally legally divorced in the United States on August 26, 1964. However, they still had a number of business ventures in common, including Jayne Mansfield Productions, the Hargitay Exercise Equipment Company, and Eastland Savings and Loan. They also co-owned the rights to *Jayne Mansfield's Wild, Wild World*, an autobiography they wrote together. Hargitay retained legal custody of their three children, even though they all lived with their mother, and a few months before Mansfield's death, he married Ellen Siano, an airline stewardess. Together, they would raise Mansfield's three middle children after her death.

After Mariska's birth, Mansfield continued to make low budget foreign films in Italy and Germany. She also recorded *Jayne Mansfield: Shakespeare, Tchaikovsky & Me* for MGM records, reciting Shakespearean sonnets, as well as poems by Browning, Wordsworth, and others. The album was not critically popular, with one reviewer calling it "30-odd poems [read] in a husky, urban, baby voice" and adding, "Miss Mansfield is a lady with apparent charms, but reading poetry is not one of them."

Though Mansfield continued to make guest appearances on various television variety shows, including *The Jack Benny Program*, *The Steve Allen Show* and *The Jackie Gleason Show*, she refused what could have become her most famous role. In 1964, CBS offered her the part of "the movie star" Ginger Grant on the new sitcom *Gilligan's Island*. Mansfield refused the role, she said, because it was too much of a stereotype she was trying to distance herself from. Instead, she went back to stage work, co-starring with Hargitay in *Bus Stop* and *Gentlemen Prefer Blondes*. *Bus Stop* was directed by Italian filmmaker Matt Cimber, and he quickly became smitten with Jayne. The two of them married on September 24, 1964 in Mexico. They had both wanted a Catholic ceremony, but no priest in the United States would marry them. Their only child, Antonio Raphael Ottaviano (Tony Cimber), was born on October 18, 1965. Following his birth, Cimber cast Mansfield in *Single Room Furnished*, and in it, her last starring role in a movie, she played three different dramatic characters. It was not widely released until after her death, but it is widely considered by critics to be her finest performance.

Following that film's completion, Mansfield had a small role in *The Las Vegas Hillbillies*, a B-grade western. She played opposite her rival, Mamie Van Doren, whom she referred to as "the drive-in's answer to Marilyn Monroe." In fact, her animosity was so strong that she refused to film their scene together, until finally, the exasperated director had to film the women separately and cut the scene together. To promote the film, Mansfield went on a cross country month long tour of the United States.

1966 proved to be one of the worst years of Mansfield's life from a personal standpoint. She was drinking heavily and cheating on Cimber with a number of men, while sometimes, during drunken fits of sadness, she would claim that she had only ever been happy with Nelson Sardelli. As soon as she filed for divorce on July 20, 1966, Mansfield moved in with Sam Brody, whom she had originally hired as an attorney. They would both get drunk and become physically violent with each other and Mansfield's oldest daughter, Jayne Marie. When Brody's wife filed for divorce, she claimed that Mansfield was the 41st woman that her husband had cheated on her with.

Then, just as she thought her life might be stabilizing, her six year old son Zoltán was attacked on November 23, 1966, by a lion while he and Mansfield were visiting Jungleland USA in California. Screaming for help, Mansfield watched as her son's entire head seemed to disappear into the lion's mouth. The child was rescued and rushed to Ventura's Community Memorial Hospital, but he had severe head trauma and would remain in the hospital for weeks. He had a six-hour surgery on his brain, plus two other operations, but just as he was beginning to recover, he came down with meningitis. In spite of all these setbacks, he eventually managed to recover, and Brody sued the park for $1.6 million before it closed down.

It was also through Brody that Mansfield discovered the Church of Satan, and she apparently pledged to join the church and displayed her framed membership certificate in her bedroom. The Church's founder, Anton LaVey, awarded her the title "High Priestess of San Francisco's Church of Satan", leading to a media frenzy and speculation that she and LaVey were having an affair. Decades later, LaVey's daughter, Karla, confirmed these rumors. Mansfield's involvement in the church remains the stuff of legends.

Not long after Zoltán recovered, Jayne appeared briefly in the comedy *A Guide for the Married Man*, and humorously, Mansfield was also listed as a technical adviser on the film. In the documentary *Spree*, which followed stars Vic Damone and Juliet Prowse through nighttime Las Vegas, Mansfield appeared in a striptease while singing "Promise Her Anything."

Chapter 8: The Actress Is Dead, Long Live the Legend

Mansfield in 1966

"Gather ye rosebuds while ye may, Old time is still a-flying:
And this same flower that smiles to-day To-morrow will be dying.

The glorious lamp of heaven, the sun, The higher he's a-getting,
The sooner will his race be run, And nearer he's to setting.

That age is best which is the first, When youth and blood are warmer;
But being spent, the worse, and worst Times still succeed the former.

Then be not coy, but use your time, And while ye may, go marry:
For having lost but once your prime You may forever tarry." - *To the Virgins, to Make Much of*

Time, by Robert Herrick, read by Mansfield on *The Joey Bishop Show* 10 days before her death.

After a tough year in 1966, it looked like Mansfield might have finally found happiness in 1967. She told one reporter, "I'd like ten more babies and ten more Chihuahuas and a few Academy Awards. Meanwhile, I enjoy being a sex symbol and making people happy." But sadly, she would have none of that. In early June 1967, Jayne Marie, who was 16 and living with her mother at that time, accused Sam Brody of physically abusing her. She contacted the Los Angeles Police Department and filed a formal complaint. Furthermore, she told the police, her mother had encouraged him to harm her. A few days later, the three appeared before a judge in juvenile court in Los Angeles. The court awarded custody of Jayne Marie to William and Mary Pique, her paternal aunt and uncle. Jayne Marie would later tell reporters that she had been disinherited by both her parents, and that she had not heard from her father since immediately after Jayne's death.

While it is difficult to believe that a woman who seemed to love her children so much could be culpable in her daughter's harm, it is important to consider the context in which the accusations were made. For one thing, Brody was just one of many men Mansfield had dragged through her daughter's life, and simply from a statistical standpoint, there was a chance that one of them would abuse Jayne Marie at some point. Furthermore, Mansfield was drinking heavily by this time, and alcohol or drug use is frequently a factor in child abuse. She was also losing her all-important looks at a time when her daughter was growing into an attractive young woman. Jayne Marie was sporting trendy mini-skirts while the great Jayne Mansfield was reduced to wearing shapeless muumuus. It's possible there was some maternal jealousy involved.

In late June 1967, Mansfield flew to Biloxi, Mississippi and moved into the Cabana Courtyard Apartments near the Gus Stevens Supper Club, where she would be performing on June 28, 1967. She had her three middle children, Miklós, Zoltán and Mariska, with her, as they were out of school for the summer and enjoying the special treat of traveling with their mother. 20 month old Tony was with his father, while Jayne Marie was with her new guardians. After her show was over, Mansfield loaded the children in the backseat of Gus Stevens' 1966 Buick Electra 225. She then climbed into the middle seat between Brody and her driver, Ronnie Harrison. She had to be on a radio show in New Orleans the next morning and hoped to get some sleep on the 90 minute trip. The tired children were soon asleep in the back seat and the car was making good speed through the dark Louisiana Low Country. It was a foggy night, a common occurrence on summer nights on the Gulf Coast. It was warm, and the men had their windows down.

Then, around 2:30 a.m. on June 29, the fog suddenly became thicker, and one of them caught a whiff of something pungent and chemical. Before either man could comment on it, there was a horrible accident. The Buick had slammed into the back of a tractor-trailer that had slowed behind a truck spraying for mosquitoes, and the car was traveling at such a speed that it actually went under the trailer, killing the three adults in the front seat instantly. Thankfully, the three children in the rear, suddenly motherless, were barely injured.

For years, rumors would circulate that Mansfield had been decapitated, but if anything, the truth might be even more gruesome. According to the policeman working the accident, "the upper portion of this white female's head was severed." More specifically, she had suffered a "crushed skull with avulsion (forcible separation or detachment) of cranium and brain." One can only imagine what the three children saw before being hustled away by the drivers of the trailer and the fogging truck. After this accident, tractor-trailers have been required to have steel underside guards on back to prevent just such accidents. They were known colloquially as Mansfield bars.

Whatever Mansfield's personal interest was in Satanism, her family handled the funeral, which was held back at home in Pen Argyl, Pennsylvania and led by the pastor of the local Zion Methodist Church, Rev. Charles Montgomery. The minister held the private service in the Pullis Funeral Home, comforting the family not with words of her fame or beauty, but with thoughts on how much she loved and cherished her elderly mother and five children. While Paul Mansfield and Matt Cimber stayed away, Mickey Hargitay attended the funeral, and, in a fit of hysteria, threw himself on her closed casket at one point. Jayne Marie was the only one of Jayne's children old enough to attend the service.

Following the funeral, Mansfield's body was buried next to her father in the Fairview Cemetery outside of Pen Argyl. Her gravestone, shaped like a heart, is inscribed "We Live to Love You More Each Day". There is also a monument to Mansfield in the Hollywood Forever Cemetery. It was erected by members of her fan club, who mistakenly listed 1938 as her year of birth.

Perhaps not surprisingly, Mansfield would not rest in peace right away, because immediately after her death, seven different people filed law suits to try to gain control of her estate, valued at about $600,000 (nearly $3.5 million in today's currency) and including the Pink Palace, her sports car and $185,000 that she inherited from Brody, assuming that he died an instant before she did. All were turned down. Then, in 1968, Jayne Marie and Matt Cimber both filed wrongful death lawsuits against the owner of the tractor-trailer.

In 1971, Sam Brody's ex-wife, Beverly, sued the estate for $325,000 that she said was the value of the gifts Sam had given Mansfield. Nearly a decade after her death, her now adult children, Jayne Marie and Mickey, as well as teenagers Zoltán and Mariska, learned that most of their mother's estate had gone to pay off her debts, including more than $10,000 in bills for lingerie and another $11,000 to plumb the famous heart-shaped pool. Hoping to cut their losses, they sold the Pink Palace to Ringo Starr, and it would later pass through the hands of Cass Elliot and Engelbert Humperdinck before being razed in 2002 to make room for a new development.

By that point, Mansfield's precious children were all grown up. Her oldest daughter, Jayne Marie, was the only one to actually grow up with her mother, since Mansfield had died when she was 16. She married in Las Vegas in 1970 and decided to follow in her mother's footsteps, becoming the first daughter of a *Playboy* playmate to appear in the magazine herself in 1976. One art historian observed, "Jayne Marie Mansfield has her mother's rounded features and mysterious eyes." She went on to appear in the magazine on several other occasions but never made it into an acting career.

While Jayne's sons had no interest in acting, her younger daughter, Mariska, has enjoyed a profitable career on both the large and small screens. She still sports a zigzag scar on the side of her head from the accident, but she has chosen not to capitalize on the memory of a mother she hardly knew. Instead, she had always been closer to the father who raised her, once saying, "My dad was Mr. Universe, so it would be fun for me to be Miss Universe." Still, she did attend her mother's alma mater, UCLA, and she entered some beauty pageants, winning Miss Beverly Hills USA in 1982. She dropped out of college before graduating and joined the Groundlings Theatre Company in Los Angeles. One of her teachers, Kathy Griffin, remembered, "We started class, and in the Groundlings curriculum, one of the first exercises you do is the cliched 'trust' game. By the time it got around to Mariska Hargitay, we'd already done it with ten or eleven students, and they had clearly gotten the point. Then it was Mariska's turn. 'Okay, Mariska, cross your arms in front of you and gently fall back,' I said. She fell back and nobody caught her. She fell flat on her ass. I was horrified. This had never happened in one of my classes before."

Since that time, Hargitay has appeared on numerous television shows, including regular roles on *Can't Hurry Love* and *ER*. She also had small roles in about a dozen movies, including *Ghoulies* and *Leaving Las Vegas*. Like her mother, she also speaks five languages: English, Hungarian, Spanish, French, and Italian. She has had an opportunity to show off her linguistic skills in her current role of Detective Olivia Benson on the long running television series *Law & Order: Special Victims Unit.*

Online Resources

Other books about Hollywood by Charles River Editors

Bibliography

Ashley, James R. The Golden Age of Hollywood Movies, 1931-1943: Vol IV Jean Harlow (2012)

Bret, David. Jean Harlow: Tarnished Angel (2009)

Golden, Eve. Platinum Girl: The Life and Legends of Jean Harlow (1991)

MacDonald, Les. Hollywood's Unhappiest Endings: Legends Never Die Updated (2013)

Marx, Samuel. Deadly Illusions: Jean Harlow and the Murder of Paul Bern (1990)

Pascal, John. The Jean Harlow Story (1964)

Rooney, Darrell and Mark A. Vieira. Harlow in Hollywood: The Blonde Bombshell in the Glamour Capital, 1928-1937 (2011)

Shulman, Irving. Jean Harlow: An Intimate Biography (1992)

Stenn, David. Bombshell: The Life and Death of Jean Harlow (2000)

Adrian, Jacob. Film Actresses Vol.6: Carole Lombard (2013)

Druxman, Michael B. Lombard (2011)

Gehring, Wes D., Ray E. Boomhower and Kathleen M. Breen Carole Lombard: The Hoosier Tornado (2003)

Harris, Warren G. Gable and Lombard (1976)

Matzen, Robert. Fireball: Carole Lombard and the Mystery of Flight 3 (2013)

Smith, Emily. The Carole Lombard Handbook

Swindell, Larry. Screwball: The Life of Carole Lombard (1975)

Cramer, Richard Ben. *Joe DiMaggio: The Hero's Life*. New York: Touchstone Press, 2000.

Dyer, Richard. "Monroe and Sexuality." *Heavenly Bodies: Film Stars and Society*. New York: Routledge, 2004. 17-63.

Haskell, Molly. *From Reverence to Rape: The Treatment of Women in the Movies*. Chicago: University of Chicago Press, 1987.

Kael, Pauline. "Marilyn: A Rip-Off With Genius." *The New York Times*. 22 Jul. 1973. From http://www.nytimes.com/books/97/05/04/reviews/mailer-marilyn.html.

Leaming, Barbara. *Marilyn Monroe*. New York: Three Rivers Press, 1998.

Margolis, Jay. *Marilyn Monroe: A Case for Murder*. Bloomington: Indiana University Press, 2011.

Naremore, James. "Marlon Brando in *On the Waterfront*." Berkeley: University of California Press, 1990. 193-212.

Rosenbaum, Jonathan. "Marilyn Monroe's Brains." *Goodbye Cinema, Hello Cinephilia*. Chicago: University of Chicago Press, 2010. 75-77.

Spoto, Donald. *Marilyn Monroe: The Biography*. New York: Cooper Square, 2001.

Taraborrelli, J. Randy. *The Secret Life of Marilyn Monroe*. New York: Grand Central Publishing, 2009.

Wolfe, Donald H. *The Last Days of Marilyn Monroe*. New York: Harper Collins, 1998.

Michael Feeney Callan (1986) Pink Goddess: The Jayne Mansfield Story. W H Allen. ISBN 978-0863791642

Mann, May (1974). Jayne Mansfield: A Biography. Abelard-Schuman. ISBN 978-0-200-72138-7.

Strait, Raymond (1974). Tragic Secret Life of Jayne Mansfield. Robert Hale. ISBN 0709155433.

Saxton, Martha (1975). Jayne Mansfield and the American Fifties. New York: Houghton Mifflin. ISBN 978-0-395-20289-0.

Luijters, Guus (June 1988). Sexbomb: The Life and Death of Jayne Mansfield. Secaucus, NJ: Citadel. ISBN 978-0-8065-1049-1.

Strait, Raymond (1992). Here They Are Jayne Mansfield. New York: S.P.I. Books. ISBN 978-1-56171-146-8.

Betrock, Alan (1993). Jayne Mansfield Vs. Mamie Van Doren: Battle of the Blondes (A Pictorial History). Shake Books. ISBN 0962683345.

Feruccio, Frank (2007). Diamonds to Dust: The Life and Death of Jayne Mansfield. Outskirts Press. ISBN 1432712411.

Jordan, Jessica Hope (2009). The Sex Goddess In American Film 1930–1965: Jean Harlow, Mae West, Lana Turner and Jayne Mansfield. Cambria Press. ISBN 978-1-60497-663-2.

Feruccio, Frank (2010). Did Success Spoil Jayne Mansfield? Her Life in Pictures & Text. Outskirts Press. ISBN 1432761234.